# A Wider Vision: A History of the World Congress of Faiths

Sixty years ago, most people viewed members of other religions with suspicion and hostility. The World Congress of Faiths, the pioneering interfaith movement founded in 1936 by the explorer and mystic Sir Francis Younghusband, has enabled a growing number of people to build bridges of friendship with members of different religious traditions. Such friendship has challenged traditional stereotypes and proved to be the basis for the growth of inter-religious understanding and co-operation across the world.

In 1936, when the WCF was founded, London was the capital of a multireligious empire. Thirty years later London itself was becoming a multireligious city. *A Wider Vision* sheds new light on the transformation of society over the last sixty years, explores key issues such as the nature of religious education in a pluralist society, interfaith worship and the role of religions in the work for world peace, and looks ahead to assess what still needs to be done.

**Marcus Braybrooke** is a well-known author in this field. He is Chairman of the World Congress of Faiths, a Trustee of the International Interfaith Centre, Oxford, of the Council for a Parliament of the World Religions, Chicago, and of the Peace Council, based in Cambridge, Wisconsin. He is also a member of the International Committee of The Temple of Understanding in New York. He is vicar of the Baldons and Nuneham Courtenay, near Oxford, where he lives with his wife, Mary. They have two grown-up children.

Other books by Marcus Braybrooke

*Be Reconciled*
*Children of One God*
*Dialogue with a Difference*
*Faith in a Global Age*
*How to Understand Judaism*
*Love without Limit*
*Pilgrimage of Hope: One Hundred Years of Global Interfaith Dialogue*
*Stepping Stones to a Global Ethic*
*Time to Meet*
*Together to the Truth*
*The Unknown Christ of Hinduism*
*Wide Embracing Love*

# A Wider Vision

A History of the World Congress of Faiths
1936–1996

Marcus Braybrooke

ONEWORLD

OXFORD

For Helen and Sarah Hobin

To my many friends in the
World Congress of Faiths

*There's a wideness in God's mercy*
*Like the wideness of the sea;*


. . .


*For the love of God is broader*
*Than the measure of man's mind*
F. W. Faber[a]

ONEWORLD
OXFORD

A Wider Vision

Oneworld Publications
(Sales and Editorial)
185 Banbury Road
Oxford OX2 7AR
England

Oneworld Publications
(US Sales Office)
PO Box 830, 21 Broadway
Rockport, MA 01966
USA

ISBN 1–85168–119–1

Printed and bound by WSOY, Finland

# Contents

# List of illustrations

# *Preface*

'I have been meeting so many of my friends' has been how I have felt as I have worked my way through the World Congress of Faiths' archives. Together with the journal, they offer a rich mine of information about the Congress, so that it has been necessary, in order to keep this book to a reasonable length, to omit much material that is of lasting interest and to pass over many names that deserve a mention. Besides this material, many of those who have been prominent in the World Congress of Faiths have themselves written books or been the subject of a biography. Even so, I hope my selection from the material will give an impression of WCF's contribution to 'learning to live as a single family',[b] which Arnold Toynbee described as a vital task of this century. Any opinions expressed are my own.

The World Congress of Faiths has remained, organizationally, quite small, but its influence has been considerable. The book shows WCF's pioneering role and also the many aspects of life to which the search for fellowship between members of the different religions is relevant. The history of WCF raises issues about the nature of inter-religious co-operation which should be of interest to all concerned for interfaith dialogue and not just to members of the Congress.

I am grateful to many people: Dr C. M. Woolgar, the archivist of the University of Southampton library and to the staff there; to the archivist of the Lambeth Palace library; to the staff of the India Office library; to Dr Edward Carpenter, a co-president of WCF, for writing a Foreword; to Brian Pearce, Jean Potter and David Storey for reading a draft of the text; to John Prickett and Tom Gulliver for sending me material and to Novin Doostdar and all the staff of Oneworld Publications for their help. I would also like to express thanks to those who have allowed me to use photographs.

I am particularly grateful to all the members of the World Congress of Faiths for creating a history about which I could write and to my wife Mary for her constant support and active involvement in the life of the Congress.

*Marcus Braybrooke*

# Foreword

There can be no question whatever that we are living in and through one of the most creative periods in the history of all religions and not least of course in Christianity. The coming together of world religions, however tentative and hesitant, is the most significant religious fact in our contemporary world society. Undoubtedly there are many who have committed themselves to this significant development of faith in all parts of the world. The World Congress of Faiths has, during its sixty years of life, devoted time, energy, thought and prayer to breaking down human barriers and working in fellowship 'nourished by spiritual experience of communion with the Ultimate'.

Amongst those who have dedicated their lives to advancing the cause of world religions is Marcus Braybrooke. Indeed he has been something of a pioneer, bold enough to face the contemporary situation with an awareness of its unique significance. And so he is eminently suited to chronicle the essentials of this influential and growing movement. He has gathered together the thinking, the feeling and the commitment of diverse persons who have concerned themselves with the relationship between the different faiths and in so doing has brought a scholarly and reflective mind to an understanding of an exciting and fast-changing period in the history of religion. This book will therefore be widely welcomed by all who are interested in contemporary religion.

It has been my privilege to know Marcus Braybrooke's work both through his writing and his activities with the World Congress of Faiths. *A Wider Vision* is but the latest of his many contributions. I am confident that his commitment will not weaken, but rather intensify as year succeeds year. Contemporary religion owes him a great debt.

The Reverend Dr Edward Carpenter
Joint president of the World Congress of Faiths

# 1. Beginnings

> . . . I dream'd
> That stone by stone I rear'd a sacred fane,
> A temple, neither Pagod, Mosque, nor Church,
> But loftier, simpler, always open-door'd
> To every breath from heaven, and Truth and Peace
> And Love and Justice came and dwelt therein.[1]

The dream that the religions of the world might become one in spirit or at least forgo prejudice and hostility and work together for a happier world is an ancient one.

One attempt to realize this vision is the World Congress of Faiths (WCF), of which this book is the story. The World Congress of Faiths, however, is built on earlier efforts to translate this dream into reality.

There are several roots from which the World Congress of Faiths was to grow. One was the Religions of Empire conference, held in London in 1924 – sometimes called a Congress of Religions – in connection with the British Empire Exhibition. A second root was the World's Parliament of Religions, held in Chicago in 1893. This inspired a (Second) Parliament of Religions in 1933, also held in Chicago, organized by the Fellowship of Faiths. A third root was the unusual spiritual experiences enjoyed by Francis Younghusband, who was to found WCF.

## The Religions of Empire conference

British society has been transformed in the sixty years during which the World Congress of Faiths has been in existence. In 1936, London was the centre of an Empire, which included people of many races and religions. Some thirty years later, Britain itself was starting to become a multiethnic and multifaith society.

Queen Victoria, in a proclamation issued in 1858 after the Indian Mutiny, outlined the imperial policy of respect for all religions:

Firmly relying ourselves on the truth of Christianity and acknowledging with gratitude the solace of religion, we disclaim alike the right and the desire to impose our convictions on any of our subjects. We declare it to be our royal will and pleasure that none be in anywise favoured, none molested or disquieted, by reason of their religion, faith or observances, but that all shall enjoy the equal and impartial protection of the law; and we do strictly charge and enjoin all those who may be in authority under us that they abstain from all interference with the religious belief or worship of any of our subjects on pain of our highest displeasure.[2]

It was during the period of Empire that a number of people in Britain began to become interested in religions other than Christianity. A considerable number of British people lived and worked in different parts of the Empire. Many took little interest in the 'natives', but some learned a lot about the languages, cultures and religions of the people amongst whom they lived. Interest was also aroused amongst supporters of the missionary work of the Church. Some Christians regarded other religions as the sphere of darkness, but some missionaries made careful studies of the religions of Asia.[3] Missionaries on furlough spoke to large numbers of congregations, many of whom gave money to support missionary work. Both the imperial and missionary interest were often from a vantage point of assumed superiority – but at least there was an interest.

The imperial context is also relevant because Francis Younghusband has been described as 'the last great imperial adventurer'.[4] Indeed, in his opening address at the Religions of Empire conference, Younghusband claimed that the ultimate basis on which the Empire would stand was religion. Indians, he said, respected Queen Victoria, because she stood for religion.[5]

The Religions of Empire conference clearly illustrates the importance to the Empire, in some people's minds, of mutual understanding between members of different religions. Ramsay MacDonald, the Prime Minister, sent a message to the conference, saying:

Many religions and many creeds live in amity within our Empire, each by their different way leading our peoples onward toward some ultimate light. I welcome cordially the objects of the conference and the knowledge which surely it spreads amongst us that our peoples, in the aspiration of the Spirit, 'walk not back to back, but with an unity of track'.[6]

Publicity for the conference made much of the fact that Christians were in a minority in the Empire. They accounted for about one sixth of the Empire's population. Of the Empire's 460 million people, about 210 million were Hindus, about 100 million were Muslims and about 12 million were Buddhists.

The conference was sponsored by the School of Oriental Studies and the Sociological Society. The organizing committee was chaired by Sir Denison Ross, director of the School of Oriental Studies in London, an expert on Oriental languages and joint author of *The Heart of Asia*. He insisted that the 'spokesman of each religion should be one who professed such religion'.[7] This gave a distinctive character to the conference and was to be copied at the World Congress of Faiths in 1936. At the conference, Sir Denison explained that:

> Up to the present if you want to know about Buddhism or Mohammedanism [the term used throughout the conference] you inevitably went to a European authority for knowledge. You may have read deeply in these religions and yet never heard a native explain the tenets of his belief and what they mean to him and the life of his people. At this conference the believer himself will lecture on his own religion.[8]

European scholars took the chair at different sessions, but were not the main speakers.

The speakers, who travelled to London from different parts of the world, were all of a high calibre. The Buddhist speakers, for example, were Dr de Silva and G. P. Malalasekera, who later became a vice-president of WCF, both from Sri Lanka (then Ceylon), and Shoson Miyamoto from Japan. Speakers included a Parsee (Zoroastrian), a Jain, a Sikh, and Hindus, including both a member of the Arya Samaj and of the Brahmo Samaj. There was a Sunni Muslim and also a Shi'ite Muslim speaker. The person who attracted greatest press attention was HH Khalifa-Tul-Masih, head of the Ahmadiyya movement in India. On arrival at

Victoria Station, as he got out of the boat train, he prayed on the platform and his call 'Allah-o-Akbur' echoed round the station. He spoke good English and gave various newspaper interviews. Whilst in Britain, he laid the foundation stone for the first mosque to be built in London, at Southfields. The Bahá'í representatives also attracted attention and there was considerable interest in this 'new' religion. It was originally hoped that Shoghi Effendi, the great-grandson of the founder, Bahá'u'lláh, and the head of the religion at that time, would himself come to London. In the event, he sent a paper which was read for him. However, Ruhi Afnan, another great-grandson of Bahá'u'lláh, did come. St Barbe Baker, who was later to found 'The Men of the Trees' and would also become a vice-president of WCF, spoke about the religion of East Africa.

The conference, as the *Evening News* put it, was for 'The Queer Religions of the Empire'.[9] There were no speakers for Judaism or Christianity. This was a deliberate decision because the organizers 'considered that their function was chiefly to familiarize those attending the lectures with the religions of the Empire relatively little known in Britain'.[10]

There was no public discussion. Sir Denison Ross had insisted that the Congress should not take 'a controversial form'.[11] All speakers from the platform were accorded equal status; they were not allowed to introduce matters that were religiously or politically controversial and all papers had to be submitted to the committee in advance.

Yet there was some controversy, partly about Younghusband's opening speech. In it, he said that 'God revealed himself in many ways, and to the followers of other religions than our own may have been revealed much of value to us'.[12] He denied preaching the equality of religions, accepting that there would always be clashes of opinion and different ways of worship. Yet he believed that all would feel actuated by a common impulse. His remarks strayed a little beyond the avowed aim of only giving information about religions and he would have liked discussion about religious truth itself. Yet providing sympathetic and accurate information, in the place of prejudicial ignorance, does itself indicate a respect for another religion. Younghusband's comments drew critical comment in some Church papers. As *The Record* put it: 'Christianity is not a competing religion among many others. It is the one and only true religion.'[13]

Following the Religions of Empire conference, Sir Denison Ross and others formed the Society for Promoting the Study of Religions. In the years prior to the meeting of the World Congress of Faiths in 1936, Sir Denison was its chairman and Sir Francis was chairman of the executive. Offices were opened at 17 Bedford Square. It was there that some years later the preparatory committee for the World Congress of Faiths would meet and there also that for some years WCF would have its office.

## The World Fellowship of Faiths

In some of the preparatory literature, the World Congress of Faiths was billed as the Second International Congress of the World Fellowship of Faiths. The World Fellowship of Faiths' First International Congress was itself also called a Second Parliament of Religions. The Second Parliament, held in Chicago in 1933, was in conscious imitation of the World's Parliament of Religions held at Chicago forty years before – so one root of WCF leads back to that landmark event.

Memories of the 1893 Parliament, which for many years was largely forgotten, have recently been revived by the celebration of its centenary. As part of the World Fair held in Chicago to mark the four hundredth anniversary of the 'discovery' of America by Christopher Columbus, a World's Parliament of Religions was held, at the suggestion of Charles Bonney. The invitation to members of all major religions to participate made the event significant. The 1893 Parliament, which I have described in *Pilgrimage of Hope*, is widely regarded as the beginning of the interfaith movement, although no continuing body was established.[14] The organization now known as the International Association for Religious Freedom was formed in 1900, although at that time it drew most of its support from Unitarians and Universalists and was only in embryonic form an interfaith organization. The International Association for the History of Religions (IAHR) held its first congress in Paris in 1901. This was devoted to the scientific and historical study of religions and at the time was for European scholars in this field.

The last day of the 1893 World's Parliament of Religions

The 1933 Parliament, still a forgotten event, was initiated by Charles Weller and Das Gupta. Weller, a social worker, started the League of Neighbors in 1918; in his words it was intended to help alien groups such as negroes and foreign-born citizens relate to American life. Das Gupta had come in 1908 from India to England, where he found little understanding of Indian culture. To help remedy this, he organized the Union of East and West, which staged a number of plays about Indian life. In 1920, Das Gupta decided to accompany Rabindranath Tagore to the United States. Das Gupta stayed on in the USA and started his Union of East and West there. Early in the 1920s he met Weller. Together they decided to merge the League of Neighbors and the Union of East and West to create the Fellowship of Faiths. This arranged meetings in several cities, at which a member of one faith paid tribute to another faith. The Fellowship also published a journal, *Appreciation*.

In May 1929, the Fellowship of Faiths arranged a meeting in Chicago on 'Peace and Brotherhood as Taught by the World's Living Faiths'. This event revived memories of the city's 1893 World's Parliament of Religions. The suggestion was made that a second parliament should be held to coincide with the Second World Fair, already being planned for 1933 to mark a 'century of progress'.

At the 1933 Parliament, which Younghusband attended,

twenty-seven gatherings were held in Chicago, with a massive total attendance of 44,000 people. Some preliminary meetings were also held in New York. Indeed, from November 1932 to May 1933, preparations centred on the New York office. The national chairman was Bishop Francis J. McConnell of the Methodist Episcopal Church. Some three hundred people agreed to serve on the national committee of what had now become the World Fellowship of Faiths. Weller and Das Gupta were the general executives. The World Fellowship of Faiths described itself as

> a movement not a machine; a sense of expanding activities, rather than an established institution, an inspiration more than an achievement. It has never sought to develop a new religion or unite divergent faiths on the basis of a least common denominator of their convictions. Instead, it believes that the desired and necessary human realization of the all-embracing spiritual Oneness of the Good Life Universal must be accompanied by the appreciation (brotherly love) for all the individualities, all the differentiations of function, by which true unity is enriched.[15]

Bishop McConnell claimed that the 1933 Parliament was an advance on the 1893 Parliament, although in my view he is not entirely fair to the latter. He argued:

> The first difference is that instead of a comparative parade of rival religions, all faiths are challenged to manifest or apply their religion by helping to solve the urgent problems which impede man's progress. The second difference is that the word 'faiths' is understood to include, not only all religions, but all types of spiritual consciousness or convictions which are determining the actual lives of significant groups of people. Educational, philanthropic, social, economic, national and political 'faiths' are thus included. The effort is to help mankind to develop a new spiritual dynamic, competent to master and reform the world.[16]

At the time the word 'faith' was used in a wider sense than 'religion', although today the two terms are sometimes used as synonyms.

Sir Francis Younghusband, in an address to the Parliament, stressed that 'the spirit of active goodwill had now to be applied on a far larger – on a worldwide – scale. Out of the very agony of war and out of the despair of economic problems we have, of set design, to make good come. Otherwise, we shall be no worthy agents of the World Spirit.'[17]

Younghusband seems to have been encouraged by the organizers to arrange the World Fellowship of Faiths' Second International Congress, held in London three years later. Das Gupta returned to Britain and regularly attended meetings of the preparatory committee for the London Congress. He soon discovered that Younghusband was used to being in charge. Indeed, one minute records that Younghusband explained that the usual practice for an international body was that whilst the general principles were adhered to, the organization was the responsibility of the national committee. This certainly was the practice of the International Association for the History of Religions until after the Second World War. It is only quite recently that air travel has made possible genuinely international planning committees.

The World Congress of Faiths of 1936 did indeed maintain the objects of the World Fellowship of Faiths. The name of the Fellowship's international president, HH the Maharaja Gaekwar of Baroda, is shown on the literature. Subsequently, the World Congress of Faiths Continuation Movement was established and WCF became an independent body. It is evident from the minutes that this caused some friction and ill feeling.

# 2. 'A Man of Action and Ideas': Francis Younghusband

'I can see Younghusband before me now, as he was at the early Congresses – always the central figure, mobile in body and mind, vibrating with energy, a perpetual stimulus,' said Lord Samuel in a broadcast he gave quite soon after Younghusband's death. There is no question that Younghusband was the moving spirit of the Congress. WCF was his 'ultimate mission. To it he devoted the remaining years of his life. He travelled about; he lectured, he enlisted much individual support among leaders of opinion in many parts of the world' – to quote Lord Samuel again.[1]

Sir John Squire, writing in *The Illustrated London News* in 1953, gave a vivid picture of how Younghusband appeared in his later years:

> To the present generation he is remembered as a short, sturdy old man, with bushy, overhanging eyebrows, clipped moustache, tight mouth, firm chin and piercing blue eyes, who took the chair on many a platform, was indisputably enthusiastic about the spiritual nature and unity of mankind and its destinies and duties in this world, but who was as lamentably lacking in eloquence in person as he was fluent, graphic and persuasive with the pen. Except in print he gave the impression – probably even when he was surmounting a peak – of being alone and retired with his thoughts.[2]

His daughter Eileen gave a rather different picture and spoke of his ability to enter into her childish enthusiasms: 'I know that when he and I were walking in mountainous country when I was a child, every plea of mine just to see what was round the next corner met with an enthusiastic response from a fellow conspirator, who also felt that what was round the next corner was far more important than that lunch was getting cold.' This sense of fun shows in many of his letters to his daughter, his 'Rogie' (a diminutive of 'little rogue'), his 'Rog Pog', 'Little Scampie' or 'Baby'.[3] His love of nature, she recalled, was not only for the great mountains but for the detailed beauty of a butterfly. '"Where's your father? Breakfast's ready": "Oh he's down the garden looking at the butterflies on the buddleia bush."'

Dame Eileen, in a talk to WCF on 16 November 1965, paid a beautiful tribute to her father:

> He was a very happy person with enormous strength and simplicity of character in the sense that he was very much a whole person with I think almost no internal conflict or guilt and very few doubts. Perhaps that is why, although I saw him angry sometimes, I never saw him in a temper or lose his temper, and certainly self-pity or conceit were very far from him. He was simple because he was single-minded, strong and clear-minded, knowing inside himself who and what he was and what he could and should do. The characteristics people most remember about him are this simplicity, happiness, vitality, an often impish sense of humour, a complete lack of pettiness because he was absorbed in things beyond himself, and over it all there was a quality of greatness. If one asks someone who knew him to describe him they will fumble with all these things and end up by saying that he was essentially childlike. And this is really it. He had the quick perception, the directness, the sense of wonder, the zest for living, the capacity for enjoyment and the sense of the ridiculous of a child.

Eileen ended her talk by saying: 'Whom the Gods love are young when they die. He was indeed young and full of happiness and confidence.'[4] To look through the minutes of both the preparatory committee and of the early years of the WCF executive is to see Younghusband's full involvement, attention to detail and youthful vigour, although he was well over seventy before the World Congress of Faiths was established.

In a broadcast, a couple of weeks before the Congress opened, Younghusband explained how he became involved:

> Fifty years ago in Manchuria I commenced a series of journeys which led me from one extremity of the Chinese Empire to the other and took me eleven times across the entire breadth of the

Himalayas from the plains of India to the plains of Turkestan and the highlands of Tibet and back. During these explorations . . . I have come into the most intimate contact with adherents of all the great religions, Hindus, Muslims, Buddhists and Confucians. I have been dependent upon them for my life . . . I have had deep converse with them on their religions, I have been invited to attend their religious ceremonies – even in the Cathedral at Lhasa. I have also been invited to speak at their religious meetings. And from all this close intercourse with men of different faiths I have derived intense enjoyment. It has forced me down to the essentials of my own Christianity and made me see a beauty there I had not till then known. It has also forced me to see a beauty in the depths of theirs. The beauty of holiness I have learned to recognise wherever found.[5]

Elsewhere he wrote:

I remember the rude Mongols far away in the midst of the Gobi Desert, setting apart in their tents the little altar at which they worshipped. I recall nights spent in the tents of wandering Kirghiz, when the family of an evening would say their prayers together. I think of the Afghan merchants visiting me in Yarkhand, and in the middle of their visits asking to be excused while they laid down a mat and repeated their prayers; of the late Mehtar of Chitral, during a morning's shooting among the mountains, halting with all his court for a few minutes to pray; and lastly of the wild men of Hunza, whom I had led up a new and difficult pass, pausing at the summit to offer a prayer of thanks, and ending with a shout of Allah.[6]

Because of his experiences, Younghusband wanted to break down the barriers that usually exist between people. Indeed, he said that the way in which everyone worked together during the blitz was creating just that sense of camaraderie at which WCF was aiming.[7]

In his address at the inaugural meeting of the WCF Paris conference, he spoke of what happened when he was run over by a car in Belgium:

A crowd with agonised expressions collected round me, showed the utmost concern for me, and did all they could to help me. And the point I wish to make is that no one enquired whether I was Aryan or non-Aryan, whether I was Belgian, French, German, Dutch or English, whether my religion was Hindu, Muslim, or Christian, and if Christian whether I was Orthodox, Catholic or Protestant. None of these questions did they ask of me. They sprang to my help because of their fellow-feeling. I was a human like themselves. What hurt me hurt them.

In the same address he went on to speak of people of unusual sensitivity who, in some crisis of their lives, become still more acutely conscious of the oneness of all being:

I personally have met several such mystics – men and women who have known what it is to be filled with a rushing mighty wind, such as the earliest Christians experienced on the day of Pentecost, and who have become intensely aware of that same unity in the spiritual world that science has established in the world of matter.

The experience, he said, was one both of unity and of joy, the two being inseparable.[8]

To those who knew Younghusband, it would have been obvious that he was speaking of his own experience, but he seems to have been careful to avoid mentioning this too publicly. In a private letter to Mary Clark of Tunbridge Wells, dated 31 May 1938, he speaks of the spiritual experience that inspired him. He begins:

I hope I am right in thinking that you have enjoyed a direct experience of God – an experience of communion with the Central Spirit of Things and have known what intensity of joy and exaltation of spirit that mystical experience brings.

Now today is my 75th birthday and it behoves me to see that in the few years to come the fullest use is made of the experience with which I have been favoured and to share with as many as possible the almost inexpressible joy which I then

Sir Francis Younghusband

felt. It is too intimate and sacred to speak of in public. Yet one would like everyone to be as convinced as one is oneself that in the Heart of Things and in the heart of every single person a Power is working not merely for 'good' but for unbelievable joy.[9]

The experience to which he refers is described in one of his books, *Vital Religion*:

> The day after leaving Lhasa I went off alone to the mountainside, and there gave myself up to all the emotions of this eventful time. Every anxiety was over – I was full of good-will as my former foes were converted into stalwart friends. But now there grew up in me something infinitely greater than mere elation and good-will. Elation grew to exultation, exultation to an exaltation which thrilled through me with overpowering intensity. I was beside myself with untellable joy. The whole world was ablaze with the same ineffable bliss that was burning within me. I felt in touch with the flaming heart of the world. What was glowing in all creation and in every single human being was a joy far beyond mere goodness as the glory of the sun is beyond the glow of a candle. A mighty joy-giving Power was at work in the world – at work in all about me and at work in every living thing. So it was revealed.
>
> Never again could I think evil. Never again could I bear enmity. Joy had begotten love.[10]

Elsewhere he mentioned other mystical experiences. The second experience was in 1905 after he had attended a Welsh revival meeting. 'I felt', he said, 'as if I were in love with every man and woman in the world.' Some twenty years later, as he described in his book *A Venture of Faith*, he again sensed the power of the Spirit. It was a 'feeling of great thankfulness. I kept muttering to myself, I thank Thee, O God, I thank Thee.'[11]

It was such mystical experiences that were to be one of the spiritual roots from which the World Congress of Faiths would grow. In some private notes, Younghusband admitted: 'I was too slow and hesitant in my middle life in developing my religious concern.'[12] Younghusband was in his seventies before he founded WCF.

## Younghusband's life

Because WCF both in its origins and throughout its history has been inspired by Younghusband's vision, some outline of his life is required. This has been told in a worthy biography by Francis Seaver and more recently in a very carefully researched and elegantly written biography by Patrick French. Both cover the many aspects of Younghusband's life.

It was perhaps fitting that Francis was born at Murree, a hill station on the north-west frontier of India. Indeed, V. Ganapathi Sastri, a devotee of Sri Ramana Maharshi, who told the Maharshi about the World Congress of Faiths, wrote to Younghusband that 'there is no doubt that in one of your previous incarnations in this planet of ours, you were an Indian'.[13]

Francis's father, John Younghusband, was in the Indian army. He taught his son to show respect to people of all races and religions.[14] His mother was Clara Jane Shaw, the sister of Robert Shaw, an explorer of Central Asia. In an interview, Younghusband spoke of his uncle's influence on him as a teenager in making him want to be an explorer.[15]

Francis, John and Clara Younghusband's second son, was born on 31 May 1863. At the age of seven months, he was taken home to Britain by his mother, who wished to care for her dying mother in Bath. After the grandmother's death, his parents returned to India, whilst Francis, now four and a half, was sent to live with his father's two unmarried sisters at Freshford. They were austere and strictly religious. Any hint of moral laxity was beaten out of him. 'They were of the sternest stuff, dressed in poke bonnets and living in the greatest simplicity. Strict teetotallers waging a war against drunkenness and teaching in the Sunday school', wrote Francis years later.

Three years later, Francis's parents returned. The reunited family moved back to Bath but the strict religious regime continued. One day Francis was found stealing a coin from a servant's purse. The punishment stressed his irredeemable wickedness and convinced him that he had betrayed his family and God: 'I lost my childhood's happiness, and became serious. Indeed I doubt if I ever completely recovered it till my old age.'[16]

In 1873, when he was ten, he travelled out to India with his parents. Three years later he returned to Britain to start at Clifton College, Bristol. There he was expected to conform to the rather conventional public-school version of Christianity. Yet already at his confirmation he was thinking for himself. He had some doubts about the virgin birth and the physical resurrection and ascension of Jesus. During this time, he paid a visit to the Alps which, he said, 'did far more for me than all the sermons I had ever heard'.[17] He was troubled by feelings that he was guilty of terrible sins – probably only masturbation. He was good at games, especially cross-country running, but too withdrawn to be popular. Clifton had a proud record of training those who would run the Empire and Francis was fitted to the mould. The poet Henry Newbolt was a contemporary and he and Francis remained friends for life.

In 1881 he entered Sandhurst. He was a solitary figure, spending his spare time reading biographies or going for long walks by himself. The only person with whom he could share his intimate feelings was his sister Emmie.

The following year he set sail for India. His choice of reading for the journey showed that already he had considerable interest in religion. Amongst many biographies, lives of Christ were prominent. He had time to think, and determined that in the future he would take nothing on authority. Ritual and dogma were unimportant. He came to think of Jesus Christ as a real man, with all the human frailties, who became great because of indomitable courage. Already his basic convictions were largely fixed. These were to develop in two main ways: in greater experience of the mystery of the universe and in broadening sympathy with, and understanding of, people of other faiths.

The highlights of the next few years of military service were his journeys of exploration to Manchuria and across the Gobi Desert. In 1888 he was granted a short leave, so that he could lecture about his travels to the Royal Geographical Society. He tried, unsuccessfully, to communicate to his parents his new sense of spiritual values. He had met and spoken with Christians of many denominations and with both educated and simple adherents of other faiths. He did not think one religion alone could be true and all others false. In the Gobi Desert, he had studied Darwin's work. He had found confirmation for his views on the gospels in Renan's *Life of Jesus* and Seeley's *Ecce Homo*. For Younghusband, at the time, the essence of Christianity was that the divine Spirit, which in Christ was a living flame, was latent in all people. All were children of the same Father and should seek to develop the divine

Spirit. Thus, by 1889, he had made his own religion for himself.[18]

On his return to India, after a time of 'arid and meaningless' soldiery, he was asked to explore all the Himalayan passes from the north. He was in his element as an explorer, but even so, during his leave in England in 1892, he again discussed with his father his project to leave the service and devote his life to the conduct of a spiritual campaign, not as an official of any Church, but in some undefined way.

In 1894 he wrote in his diary: 'I think I have had from time to time the feeling that I was born to recognise the divine spark within me . . . I shall through my life be carrying out God's Divine message to mankind.' A little after this entry, he was thrown from his horse and lay unconscious for fourteen hours. As he recovered, he read Leo Tolstoy's *The Kingdom of God is Within You* – a book which deeply impressed him and was also to influence Mahatma Gandhi greatly. Younghusband had been reading books on evolution by Herbert Spencer, who almost convinced him but did not inspire him. Tolstoy made his heart leap. On 31 August 1894, he wrote in his diary:

> It has influenced me profoundly . . . I now thoroughly see the truth of Tolstoy's argument that Government, capital and private property are evils. We ought to devote ourselves to carrying out Christ's saying, to love one another (not engage in wars and preparation for wars and not resist evil with evil).
>
> Tolstoy does not say how society can exist without Govt, capital and private property but he says the few great ones, like Columbus, must plunge into the unknown and discover the way. And this is what I mean to do. To set the example first of all by giving up Govt service and all my private property except what is absolutely necessary for supporting life.[19]

A few days later, he sent a letter to the government explaining his intentions. Almost immediately, however, he was to meet with George Curzon, who was visiting India. By the end of the year Younghusband was back in Britain on leave and quite quickly recovered his health and good spirits. Plans to get rid of his possessions were put to one side. He was still unsure about his future. His father suggested a return to government service, whilst others thought he should try journalism or business. He was also doing preliminary work on a book, *The Heart of a Continent*.

Disturbing developments on the frontier at Chitral justified his warnings about the instability there. A speech he gave on the issue at the Royal Geographical Society on 25 March 1895 was fully reported in *The Times*, which invited him to return to Chitral as its special correspondent. By 21 April, Younghusband was riding back into Chitrali territory.

Patrick French describes him in early 1895:

> Frank Younghusband presents a puzzling spectacle at this stage of his career. Profoundly moved by the writings of Leo Tolstoy, he has quit government service in order to devote his life to God. Instead he falls into a job as a journalist and public speaker, anxiously defending a 'forward' policy in the Great Game [the competition between Russia and Britain in Central Asia]. The summer of 1895 finds him living with his old father in Southsea, aged thirty-two, with little money, thinning hair, few definite prospects and a vague wish to find 'that form of religion which is best adapted to the men of the present day and which would form the religion of the future'. At the same time he has recovered a certain social confidence.[20]

Younghusband had for some time had an epistolary romance with a married woman, Nellie Douglas. This was brought to an end by the fact that on returning to South Africa, where he had been sent by *The Times*, he had fallen in love with, and intended to marry, Helen Magniac. She had been brought up in a wealthy home and her family had aristocratic links. Her father, who died in 1891, had speculated on the Stock Exchange and left massive debts. The family was forced to sell Chesterfield House and its contents. Helen was afraid of the sexual aspect of marriage and Francis agreed to a marriage without sex. The agreement must have been quite quickly broken, as Helen was pregnant within the year. Even so, it was never a fulfilling marriage for either of them. Younghusband tried to do his duty to his wife and, wherever he was, wrote regular letters to her. She did not share his many ventures and at the end of her life was in a nursing home in

London. The marriage was also too much for Younghusband's sister Emmie, who could not bear another woman to replace her in her brother's affections. Emmie was to become the victim of mental illness and depression.

The wedding took place on 11 August 1897, and was followed by a month's honeymoon in Paris. Now needing a steady career, Younghusband, with Helen, returned to India. He hoped to rejoin the government of India's political department. Instead he was given the lowly position of Third Assistant to the Political Agent in Rajputana. The Political Agent's job was to advise – a polite word for 'control' – a prince who, recognizing British suzerainty, ruled one of the many states of India. Younghusband was posted to the hill station of Mt Abu. There, Charles, their first child, was born but died as a tiny baby. Helen was crushed by grief. The time at Mt Abu was not a happy one for the young couple.

Strangely, Mt Abu has more recently come to play a part in the story of WCF. This hill town is the headquarters of the Brahma Kumaris, who have built their World Spiritual University there. In recent years the Brahma Kumaris movement has given active support to WCF and other interfaith work. It was at their Global Co-operation House in London that the 1993 Year of Inter-religious Co-operation and Understanding was launched.

With Lord Curzon's appointment as Viceroy of India in 1899, Younghusband's prospects began to improve, as the two were already friends and political allies. In 1903, Younghusband was asked by Lord Curzon to lead a mission to Tibet. This was a difficult and dangerous undertaking. Controversy has continued to surround what happened. At Lhasa, where he met the Dalai Lama's regent, he successfully signed a treaty, but his work was repudiated by the politicians. It was as he was leaving Lhasa that he had the decisive spiritual experience which has already been described.

On his return to Britain after the Tibetan venture, Younghusband was regarded as a hero, except by Whitehall. In 1906, he returned to India to become British Resident in Kashmir. The following year his father died. He felt his loss acutely, but also felt free to pursue a spiritual mission. In 1908, he drafted a letter to the poet Henry Newbolt about his 'important mission': 'For years past I have felt there is something wrong with our present religion . . . Christianity itself is puny and childish.'[21] When in 1908 the job as Commissioner of the Frontier Provinces, for which he had been hoping, went to a rival, Younghusband decided the time had come to leave India.

In December 1909, he sailed from Bombay. It would be nearly thirty years before he returned to Asia. Immediately on his return to Britain, he involved himself in the first 1910 general election campaign and again in the second campaign at the end of that year. Besides making a number of speeches, he wrote some articles for the press as well as two books, *Kashmir* and *India and Tibet*.

His mind was still brooding on religious matters. In an article in the *National Review*, he wrote: 'Behind all political effort and social endeavour must be the impulse which religion alone could give. It was for the renewal and revitalizing of our religion that the English people really craved.'[22] Already for some fifteen years, religion had been Francis Younghusband's primary interest. He was aware of the higher-critical study of the scriptures and of scientific advance. As a result he was dissatisfied with the conventional religion in which he had been brought up. 'I had visions of a far greater religion yet to be, and of a God as much greater than our English God as a Himalayan giant is greater than an English hill.'[23]

Already he wished to communicate this 'greater religion' but he knew that first he had to clarify the intellectual framework of his conception of the universe. Convinced that the universe was governed by its own laws and not by external interference, he continued his study of science. A variety of experiences and his reading of nature-mystics, such as Blake and Wordsworth, made him dissatisfied with some scientists' 'petty-minded hatred of religion'. A study of McTaggart's *Some Dogmas of Religion* and *Studies in Hegelian Cosmology* led him to seek the acquaintance of the author, who was an Old Cliftonian.

Having tested his faith against intellectual criticism, he set to work to give it shape and definition in a book to be called *The Inherent Impulse*. As the work was nearing completion, he met, whilst in Belgium, with an accident, which was followed by prolonged illness. This experience led him to revise his book, which, eventually, was published in the autumn of 1912, with the title *Within*. This was the first of several books in which he described his religious views.

In October 1914, his *Mutual Influence*, which was his most humanist book, was published, but it did not sell many copies. When war broke out, Younghusband offered his services to the India Office and then to the War Office. Both offers were declined. In 1915, he was asked to take an unpaid job at the India Office preparing daily news telegrams for the Viceroy on the progress of the war. These were then used for official news releases to the Indian press. Later that year, he caught the mood of the nation in a letter to the *Daily Telegraph*, saying: 'We are engaged in a spiritual conflict – a holy war – the Fight for Right.'[24] Fight for Right quickly became a movement to bolster public morale, and Younghusband toured the country giving speeches. In 1917, he was made a Knight Commander of the Star of India. Soon, however, Fight for Right fell apart as divisions between idealists and jingoists came to the surface.

For the last months of the war, Younghusband gave his time to thinking about India and the constitutional changes that should be introduced after the end of the war. He prefaced his memorandum with a recommendation that reform be instituted in the express context of future self-determination and be accompanied by an affirmation of belief in those spiritual values that in India bulk larger than politics.

After the war, Younghusband in effect lived two lives. One was with his establishment friends, many of whom showed no interest in his religious views. In the 1920s he was involved in many societies; as president of the Royal Geographical Society he initiated and backed Mallory's attempt to conquer Mt Everest.

In his other life he was exploring spiritual ideas both with his religious friends and in his writings. In 1921, he wrote *The Heart of Nature; or The Quest for Natural Beauty* which is broken up into alternate chapters of description and philosophizing. In 1923, he wrote *The Gleam*, an account of the life of the pseudonymous Nija Svabhava. The real hero, of course, was Younghusband, and he nearly revealed this in a letter to *The Times*, but prevented its publication at the last minute. His next religious book was *Mother World (in Travail for the Christ that is to be)*. In it, he speaks of

Mother Nature and talks of the world as a benevolent deity. His pantheistic tendencies were attacked by *The Tablet*. The book ends with the belief that the world was 'groaning and travailing to bring forth a leader', the 'Christ that is to be', the God-child that Younghusband had first prophesied in *Within*.[25]

Amongst the societies that he supported was one to encourage religious drama (now Radius). He was also keen to promote a knowledge of the world's religions. He was, as we have seen, active in support of the Religions of Empire conference and the Society for Promoting the Study of Religions and then of the World Fellowship of Faiths. It was, however, to the World Congress of Faiths that he devoted the main energy of his final years.

Sir John Squire wrote that to define Younghusband's religion would be hopeless:

> Sometimes he seemed a Pantheist, sometimes a pure monotheist of the Mohammedan or Jewish kind. He regarded himself as a loyal member of the Church of England and was a zealous attendant at Divine Service; yet with his views about the impersonality of the deity and the mere surpassing human goodness of Christ, he can hardly have taken the Apostles' Creed literally. The one thing certain is that he 'walked with God daily' and that his working philosophy did make him continually aware of his responsibility to 'the power, not ourselves, making for righteousness'.[26]

K. D. D. Henderson, who was secretary of the Spalding Trust, wrote:

> The basis of his heresy was the conviction that the message of Jesus Christ depended for its efficacy upon his humanity. He [Jesus] attained to a higher level of being than any other man, and provided for posterity an example at which to aim. The force of this example fell to the ground if you postulated in him any element whatsoever of the super-human. Christianity has survived by virtue of his personality, perpetually shining out from the gospel narratives with an intensity and vitality approached by none of his interpreters, not even by John or Paul.

Younghusband found in Jesus an embodiment of a Love elemental rather than personal, an all-loving universal power, and he was as impatient of the ritualist approach to God as he was of attempts to define God's essence or prove his existence by argument. His practical philosophy was 'to show forth Thy praise not only with our lips but in our lives, by giving up ourselves to thy service'.

'No one who has seen what I have seen', he wrote in 1892, 'and still more surely no one who has been influenced as I have been, can doubt that there must be an all-pervading spirit in nature, and this spirit is God; and the essence of the spirit is Love.'[27]

Younghusband's basic conviction was that joy was the ground and crown of all religion. Joy, he claimed, was at the heart of Christ's message. Hindu, Buddhist and Muslim saints had declared the same, and the Psalms were full of its expression. Although love was usually regarded as more fundamental, he held that joy was both deeper and higher. This emphasis did not mean that he disregarded evil and suffering. He believed, however, that the joy of life not merely counterbalanced the suffering and wickedness but could transform it into good.

This emphasis on joy is clear in the review he wrote during the last year of his life, of Sri Aurobindo's *The Life Divine*:

Bliss is the object of the Creator in creating . . . Bliss is the motive power of the whole universe. He who has once reached the culmination of the Spirit will be moved with pity and compassion for the sufferings of his fellows both bodily and spiritual. He will love them and sympathize with them. He will be filled with something far more deeply penetrating than love and sympathy. He will see and feel the Divine in all forms – animal as well as human. The Divine in them will touch the Divine in himself, till the joy that is in him will remain with them that their joy may be full.[28]

It is important to recognize that Younghusband's conception of a fellowship of faiths sprang from a mystical sense of the unity of all people. As George Harrison put it: 'Sir Francis believed in divine fellowship. Every single man is bound up with every other man and with all living creatures, and with the entire physical universe in one mighty whole.'[29] The 'brotherhood of man' was for Younghusband not a religious slogan but a truth realized in religious experience. In such an experience, a person is 'lifted right out of himself and wafted up to unbelievable heights. He seems to expand to infinite distance and embrace the whole world.'[30]

'The ultimate aim of the Fellowship can only be to intensify our sense of kinship with the universe to the mystic degree – to that point when the individual feels as if he and the universe were madly in love with one another,' Younghusband said in a talk at Westerham in Kent.[31]

In his later working for the World Congress of Faiths, Younghusband made it clear that there was no intention of formulating another eclectic religion. He rather aimed to help members of all faiths to become aware of the universal experience that had been his. The Congress, he hoped, 'would awaken a wider consciousness and afford men a vision of a happier world-order in which the roots of fellowship would strike down deep to the Central Source of all spiritual loveliness till what had begun as human would flower as divine'.[32] The human fellowship that he sought to promote was inextricably linked to communion with the divine. The Congress, therefore, was an attempt to give practical expression to the mystic's vision of unity.

# 3. 'World Fellowship through Religion': the 1936 Congress

## 1934–6

Formal preparations for the World Congress of Faiths began on 16 November 1934 – exactly four years before I was born.

Younghusband had no illusions about the size and complexity of the task: 'Make the creation of a world fellowship a great adventure, a most difficult and heroic task requiring all the manliness, courage, skill, equanimity of any great military or exploring adventure,' he jotted down in his notebook on Christmas Day 1934.[1] This notebook, in which Younghusband wrote down ideas as they came to him and in which he planned out meetings, illuminates the more official records contained in the minutes of various committee meetings.

The minutes of the first meeting make clear the link with the World Fellowship of Faiths, which had arranged the Second World's Parliament of Religions in Chicago in 1933. At the first meeting, the short title 'International Congress of Faiths' was adopted. On 12 September 1935, it was suggested that this be changed to World Congress of Faiths, with the subtitle 'Fellowship through Religion'. After conversation with Dr Das Gupta, one of the organizers of the 1933 Chicago gathering, it was agreed that the title of the Congress be 'The World Congress of Faiths, being the Second International Congress of the World Fellowship of Faiths'.

The name 'World Congress of Faiths' has survived – an alternative at the time was 'The All Faiths Fellowship'. It has sometimes been considered misleading and alternatives have been suggested. Despite Younghusband's hopes, WCF is not really a world body, but rather a British-based organization, although it has an international influence and readership of its journal, *World Faiths Encounter*, is scattered across the world. 'Congress of World Faiths' might be a better name. For a time, the subtitle 'The Inter-Faith Fellowship' was given prominence on the notepaper. The use of initials, WCF, can hide precision of meaning. The name has survived partly because it is known in various reference books

*Nov. 16. 1934.*

A Meeting was held on the 16ᵗʰ November, 1934,
at 2·30 p.m. at 9 Arlington Street, S.W.I. The
following members attended:-

Sir Francis Younghusband, Miss Winifred
Wranch, Miss Beatrix Holmes, Dr. Prynce Hopkins, Mrs.
Alexander, Mrs. Williams, Miss Sharples, Mr. Kedarnath Dasgupta,
Mr. Jackman, my Stanley Rice.
The proceedings commenced with a few
minutes' silence for spiritual communion. The Chairman
referred to the spiritual aims of the Fellowship in his
opening remarks.

The short title, "International Congress of
Faiths", was adopted.

Dr. Hopkins suggested some names of well-known
authors, who could be asked to join the Council
or address the Congress.

The Press communiqué, written by the Chairman
was approved. It was resolved that it should be
sent to the principal newspapers in England and
other countries.

Miss Holmes was asked to prepare a list
of the societies and associations that should be
invited to send delegates to the Congress.

Minutes of the first meeting of the World Congress of Faiths

and partly because human inertia has avoided the legal efforts
necessary to change a name and a constitution, but nor has anyone
come up with a more compelling name.

The first meeting of the executive took steps to establish a
national council. It was also soon agreed that all who contributed
£1 should be considered members of the Congress, and that an
international council should be established. The original plan was
to have the first part of the Congress in London and then to move
to Oxford, where the conference would become residential. By

early 1935, it had been agreed that the Congress should be in July 1936.

At the meeting of the national council on 27 February 1935, Younghusband explained that three main ideas were to be taken over from the Second Chicago World's Parliament of Religions:

1. Working for world fellowship.
2. Welcoming the necessary differences among fellows in any fellowship.
3. Uniting the inspiration of all faiths upon the solution of man's present problems.[2]

At the same meeting, Younghusband also explained the executive's proposal that the subject should be 'World Fellowship through Religion'. He introduced a statement, which still has contemporary resonance, of the hindrances and aids to the achievement of fellowship:

Hindrances:
1. Fear, suspicion, hatred and other forms of spiritual instability which lead to wars between nations and conflicts between individuals;
2. Nationalism in excess or defeat;
3. Racial Antagonism and Race Domination;
4. Religious Differentiation;
5. Class Domination;
6. Poverty;
7. Ignorance.

Aids to the achievement of fellowship:
1. Education (Literary, Scientific, Philosophic or Religious);
2. Improved economic conditions;
3. Drama, Music or other forms of art;
4. Examples of saintly and heroic lives held up for emulation;
5. Prayer;
6. Concentrated Meditation on the Supremely perfect things in life;
7. Sharing spiritual experiences;

8. common pursuit of truth, common enjoyment of beauty, common worship of a God common to all mankind. Common deeds of charity.[3]

The minutes for the meeting on 4 April illustrate the varying reactions of the Anglican clergy to the proposal. The chairman reported on an interview he had had with the Archbishop of Canterbury and read the letter he had received. This explained that the Archbishop was unable to accept an invitation to be president of the Congress. As the next item of business, however, Younghusband announced that the Dean and Chapter of St Paul's Cathedral would be glad to welcome members of the Congress to a service there.

I have not been able to find the Archbishop's letter. The Lambeth Palace archives, however, contain correspondence from Buckingham Palace asking Archbishop Cosmo Gordon Lang's advice. The first letter asked how the Archbishop thought King Edward VIII should reply to Sir Francis Younghusband's request that he should preside at the opening session of the Congress. Lang, in his reply to Commander Campbell, said that he had told Younghusband that he personally could not take part in the Congress 'for the reason that this might be taken to imply that I thought Christianity was only one of many religions in spite of being as I believed the true religion based upon Divine Revelation'. Although, as the Archbishop admitted, some respectable Church of England clergy had given the Congress their sanction, he concluded that 'I am disposed to think His Royal Highness might well decline the invitation'.[4]

In the middle of June, the Palace again asked for the Archbishop's advice. This time the question was whether the King should accept a telegram of loyal greetings and send a reply. Lang, this time, was more amenable. 'The Christian religion,' he wrote, 'while having much in common with other great world religions, is unique in that it is based on a specific Divine revelation.' Nonetheless, those attending the Congress were people of 'the highest respectability'. Lang, therefore, thought that if the King was sent a telegram, there was 'no reason why His Majesty should not send a reply in a guarded form'. The message, preserved in the WCF archives, expresses thanks for the greetings of the Congress

**BUCKINGHAM PALACE**

I am much gratified to receive the message
which Your Highness has sent me on behalf of those
attending the World Congress of Faiths.  Please express to
them my sincere thanks.

I earnestly hope that the deliberations of
the Congress may help to strengthen the spirit of peace
and good-will on which the well-being of mankind depends.

RDWARD R.I.

3rd. July, 1936.

A message from Edward VIII to the Maharaja Gaekwar of Baroda,
president of the 1936 World Congress of Faiths

and continues: 'I earnestly hope that the deliberations of the
Congress may help to strengthen the spirit of peace and good-will
on which the well-being of mankind depends.'[5]

The Lambeth archive also contains a pamphlet, *World
Fellowship through Religion*, written by the Revd O.
Younghusband, a cousin of Sir Francis, which asks why no bishop

of the Church of England attended the Congress. For Sir Francis too it remained a puzzle and a disappointment that so few leading members of the Church of England gave the Congress their backing. The only Anglicans on the Council in 1939 were the Deans of St Paul's and of Canterbury, Canon Raven, Dr Major and Archdeacon Townshend.

The office of the preparatory committee was established at Bedford Square, in the offices of the Society for Promoting the Study of Religions. Much of the detailed office work was done by Beatrix Holmes, whom Younghusband described as 'the maid-of-all-work of the WCF'. Arthur Jackman was appointed as 'organising secretary', at a salary of £350 per annum. Jackman had close links with the Theosophical Society. In earlier days, Younghusband had been critical of theosophy, which he described as a doctrine for 'neurotic and partially educated ladies'. Jackman was to play an important part in the life of WCF until the late forties. It seems that he and Younghusband did not always agree – indeed Younghusband wrote of himself being 'constantly hindered' by Jackman and the executive committee. Patrick French also observes that there was a split between idealists and the groupies: the leading public supporters such as Gilbert Murray and Herbert Samuel had an interfaith agenda, but many of the office volunteers were simply fans of Younghusband. Personally he was devoted to the aim of religious fellowship, yet craved the praise and support of his admirers. As he wrote to Helen, his wife: 'It is quite wonderful what appreciation I am getting – far better than any peerages and things.'[6]

George Bernard Shaw's response to Younghusband's request for support is worth recording. Shaw admitted that he 'had found in the east a quality of religion which is lacking in these islands', but he doubted the practicality of uniting 'men of burning faith'. He believed all potential members should be asked a number of questions, including: '1. On what public grounds would you shoot your next door neighbour, excluding those already recognised by our criminal court?' Shaw believed that talk of faith and love and unity was all very well, but that spiritual types were 'extraordinarily quarrelsome'. 'Get them round a table to agree on a basic manifesto or spend half a crown of public money, and most of them will make frantic scenes and dash out of the room after hurling their resignations at you.'[7] I recall Lady Norman saying after one WCF executive meeting that if you want an unholy row join a religious committee!

## The Congress

The Congress was held at University College, London, from 3 to 8 July 1936. It was not residential, and this restricted the social intercourse between participants, but discussion was encouraged and was carried on with good humour. The chairmen and leaders of debate were carefully chosen. Younghusband persuaded a galaxy of distinguished scholars to speak. It is interesting that the speakers, for the most part, were scholars rather than religious leaders.

The first speaker was Yusuf Ali, principal of the Islamic College at Lahore and a translator of the Qur'an into English. He spoke of the revolution in communications which was making the world one, but he was equally aware of the deep divisions in the world. He then spoke of his own friendships with members of different religions: 'Thus you will see that, individually, many of us have actually felt and experienced the fellowship of faiths. Why can we not bring it about on a larger scale and in a more organised way? . . . The office of Religion is to bind us together in the bonds of a common humanity.'[8]

The second speaker was Dr D. T. Suzuki, whose master had attended the 1893 World's Parliament of Religions. Suzuki was professor of Buddhist philosophy at Otani University, Kyoto, and his books on Zen Buddhism were widely read in the West. His was a scholarly talk about ignorance and *karma*, with a careful explanation of the meaning of *Sunyata* or 'Emptiness'. His closing remarks, in the face of the rise of Fascism in many parts of the world, including his own country, were almost despairing:

If it is impossible for us, advocating the various faiths of the world, to stem the tide even when we know where it is finally tending, the only thing we can do is to preserve a little corner somewhere on earth, east or west, where our faiths can be safely guarded from utter destruction. When all the turmoils

are over . . . we may begin to think seriously of the folly we
have so senselessly been given up to, and seek the little corner
we have saved for this purpose. . . . That at present no nations
are willing to have a world religious conference positively
demonstrates the truth that our Karma-hindrance still weighs
on us too heavily.[9]

Another Buddhist, Professor Malalasekera, from Sri Lanka,
outlined the Buddha's teaching on the Four Noble Truths. He
suggested that the promotion of fellowship depended on personal
growth.

Professor Nicolas Berdiaeff (as his name is spelt in the
proceedings although Nicolai Berdyaev may be the more
familiar spelling), an eminent philosopher, echoed Suzuki's sense
of impending doom. Berdiaeff had suffered several terms of
imprisonment after the Russian Revolution and was exiled from
Russia in 1922. 'We live in a cruel, inhuman epoch, when hatred
and dissension are rife among nations, states and social classes,' he
began. Religion had itself been a major cause of discord and
dissension. 'Religious fanaticism is one of the most serious
deformations of human nature.' In such a divided world, the
spiritual integration of Europe and the world was essential. He
argued from Christian sources for co-operation with members of
other religions. 'Certain Catholic theologians', he said, 'make a
distinction between the soul and the body of the Church; they
consider as the body those who formally belong to the
organisation of the Church . . . and they include in the soul those
who, without being members of the Church, direct their thoughts
towards God and the divine, towards truth and goodness.' Good
Hindus and Buddhists belong to the true Church[10] – a view which
foreshadows both the generosity and condescension of talk of
'anonymous Christians'.

Stressing Christianity's commitment to a true humanism,
Berdiaeff called on the Christian conscience to demand a radical
change in relations between the peoples of the world. In face of
hostility and hatred in the world, 'it is the duty of the religions to
struggle for the brotherhood of man, for the unity of mankind'
and 'for the dignity of all human beings as children of God'. Such
unity, he suggested, will not come by intellectual or doctrinal

Dr D. T. Suzuki

agreement, but out of real spiritual experience of brotherhood and
charity.

The two best-known Hindu speakers were Sir Sarvepalli
Radhakrishnan and Dr S. N. Das Gupta, author of *A History of
Indian Philosophy*. Dr Radhakrishnan was about to take up the
Spalding Chair of Eastern Religion and Ethics at Oxford and was
to be a future president of India. He studied for a time at Madras

Sir Sarvepalli Radhakrishnan

Christian College. When I went there as a student, my professor, Dr C. T. K. Chari, arranged with his brother C. T. Venugopal for me to be received by Dr Radhakrishnan, who was then president of India, at Raj Bhavan. I still recall the president's graciousness and that he walked with us to the door. Later, I was to invite him to become patron of the World Congress of Faiths, which he accepted. In the early days of WCF, he served on the committee. Radhakrishnan did much to popularize Vedanta in the West and wrote with great elegance. It took western students some time to realize the enormous variety of Hinduism and to discover that not all Hindus shared Radhakrishnan's Idealist philosophy.

Radhakrishnan had a great sense of the need for spiritual unity to match the growing physical unity of the world: 'Those who believe in humanity and in the power of the spirit to realise ideals must prepare the minds of men for the new world order.' Religions, however, had failed, being often a cause of division rather than a force for unity. The mistake had been to claim finality for certain creeds and doctrines. Spiritual experience goes beyond human descriptions of it. 'When the finite man enters the Divine presence, he discards all images and enters naked, Alone with the Alone . . . The Supreme . . . is grasped as the central reality in the moments of our deepest life and experience.' This view has been widely influential amongst members of WCF, especially in its early days. The claim is that religious differences are at a cultural and intellectual level, whereas the experience of the divine is essentially the same. In this way Absolutist and Personal concepts of the Ultimate are reconciled. Yet, Radhakrishnan argued, human beings cannot dispense with symbols and create a purely spiritual religion.[11]

The Congress, he said, did not ask anyone to change their religion. Each had a contribution to make. What was needed was spiritual evolution and a recognition of spiritual unity:

> Fellowship of faiths which implies appreciation of other faiths is no easy indulgence of error and weakness or lazy indifference to the issues involved. It is not the intellectual's taste for moderation or the highbrow's dislike for dogma. It is not the politician's love for compromise or being all things to all men, nor is it simply a negative freedom from antipathies. It is understanding, insight, full trust in the basic reality which feeds all faiths and its power to lead us to the truth. It believes in the deeper religion of the Spirit which will be adequate for all people, vital enough to strike deep roots, powerful to unify each individual in himself and bind us all together by the realisation of our common condition and common goal.[11]

As a student at Madras Christian College, in my attempt to study

Hindu philosophy I relied on both Dr Radhakrishnan's writings and also Professor S. N. Das Gupta's *History of Indian Philosophy*. I also had the privilege in Lucknow of meeting some of those who had worked closely with Das Gupta. I have on my shelves a little book of his, *The Fundamentals of Indian Art*. I was interested to find that he began by talking about art and its relationship to religion; both point to the spiritual reality of human nature. Art, Das Gupta said, encourages sympathy with other people and with nature, just as religion should. World Fellowship through Religion would come, he argued, by spiritual awakening:

> All forms of Hindu religion mean a spiritual awakening of the nature in man through an internal transformation of personality, just as art in its varied forms means the creative transformation of a sensuous content for the revelation of the spirit in nature and man. The fellowship of man and the awakening of the spirit are thus the two poles that have determined all religious movements in India.[12]

Another Hindu speaker at the Congress was Professor Mahendra Nath Sircar of Calcutta, who stressed the value of silence in the spiritual life. Other speakers at the Congress included Ranjee G. Shahani, Walter Johannes Stein, editor of *The Present Age*, and the novelist Jean Schlumberger. Professor Marcault of the University of Grenoble stressed the importance of education. A paper on science and religion which Professor Haldane had written before his death was read.

One of the Jewish speakers, Professor J. L. Magnes, president of the Hebrew University, asked whether it was possible to make fellowship in times of war: 'What could we do during the coming war?' He questioned religions' readiness to endorse war and called for a fellowship of those who believe no war is righteous, even though they participate in what they believe to be a necessary war. 'I regret that in what I have said there is no high note of hope, but only the prospect of dull resistance. In a spirit of deep pessimism I have merely talked of preparing a lowly fellowship of the spirit for use during the coming war.'[13]

Shoghi Effendi, the head of the Bahá'ís, sent a paper that was read for him. This outlined Bahá'u'lláh's Ground Plan of World Fellowship. Bahá'u'lláh taught that religions are one at heart. He recognized that all religious teachers were prophets of God. It was through religion, Shoghi Effendi argued, that humanity will be rescued from dissension and united in a fellowship of hearts.

Islam's emphasis on tolerance and respect for other faiths was described in a careful exposition by Sir Abdul Qadir, a High Court judge and a member of the council of the Secretary of State for India. Islam, he pointed out, means 'Peace'. He tried to dispel misunderstandings of *Jihad*, which is often translated as 'Holy War'. Another Muslim was Sheikh Mohammed Mustapha al-Maraghi, rector of Al-Azhar University in Cairo and ex-Grand Cadi of the Sudan. He stressed that fellowship among people of religion has to precede universal fellowship. He suggested creating a body to cleanse religious consciousness of hatred and jealousy and to strengthen religious awareness, especially amongst the intellectual classes. Professor Louis Massignon, a scholar on Islam from the Sorbonne, also read a paper. Another speaker was Sirdar Mohan Singh, from the Punjab. S. I. Hsiung gave a talk on the teachings of Confucius.

Christian speakers were Dr J. S. Whale, president of Cheshunt College, Cambridge, and the Revd P. T. R. Kirk, who was director of the Industrial Christian Fellowship. Whale spoke about aspects of modern life and its challenge to religion – with, in parenthesis, a side-swipe at syncretism. Kirk concentrated on the economic barriers to peace.

Many of the published papers are of a high quality. Of greatest interest, perhaps, is the different attitudes they display towards the relationship of religions to each other. On the one hand, the Revd P. T. R. Kirk claimed that Christianity must be accepted by the whole of mankind, and Moulvri A. R. Dard made a similar claim for the Ahmadiyya community. By contrast, the paper prepared by Professor Haldane included this passage:

> Many Christians entertain the ideal of converting non-Christian peoples to Christianity. I think that a much higher ideal is to understand and enter into sympathy with the religions which exist in other countries and to use this understanding and sympathy as a basis for higher religion.[14]

Several speakers, such as the Chief Rabbi and Canon Barry, stressed the differences between religions, whereas Ranjee G. Shahani said the differences were trivial: 'Jesus and Buddha, Shakespeare and Ramakrishna – are in essence "members one of another".'[15]

In general it was agreed that the aim of the Congress was not to create one new synthetic religion, but to generate understanding and a sense of unity between the religions of the world. Rabbi Dr Israel Mattuck, chairman of the executive of the World Union for Progressive Judaism, put it like this:

> I am not pleading for one religion to include all men. I like diversity. I should no more want a world with one religion than I should want only one coloured rose in my garden. But we can have diversity without enmity and when we do this, I believe, the world will be more ready to receive our message about human unity and human peace.[16]

Several speakers hoped that the world religions could together work for peace and spiritual uplift. Professor Marcault, a French professor of psychology, highlighted the important question of what in practice religions can actually do together. It is not easy to find areas of practical co-operation in which to give concrete expression to the desire to work together. 'Peace and fellowship', he said, 'can only be constructive if they are incarnated in some positive religious aim in whose realization all faiths can agree to cooperate, and whose universality maintains them united.'[17]

In his foreword to the published papers, *Faiths and Fellowship*, Sir Francis Younghusband stressed again that the one aim of the Congress was to promote the spirit of fellowship. He ruled out certain misunderstandings. There was no intention of formulating another eclectic religion, nor of seeking the lowest common denominator, nor of appraising the value of existing religions and discussing respective merits and defects. It was not maintained that all religions are the same, nor equally true, nor as good as one another. The hope was to 'intensify that sense of community which is latent in all men' and to awaken a livelier world-consciousness. Younghusband mentioned that, through discussion and reflection, the conception of God grew greater, and that by coming closer to each other, members of different religions deepened their own spiritual communion.

The chair was taken by distinguished scholars, such as Sir E. Denison Ross and Professor H. G. Wood or leading figures, such as the Chief Rabbi, the Aga Khan, Dr C. E. M. Joad and Lord Samuel. Two women were asked to chair sessions: Dame Elizabeth Cadbury and Dame Ogilvie Gordon.

In the evenings there were public meetings. There were also devotional times, led by members of different faiths. These included a Jewish service, led by Rabbi Leslie Edgar, and a Coptic service. Members of the Congress were also invited to services at St Paul's Cathedral and at Canterbury Cathedral. The government provided a reception at Lancaster House and Sir Francis Younghusband hosted one at the Royal Geographical Society.

Press coverage was mixed. Some letters about the Congress were very hostile, with talk of heathen temples and idols. *The Inquirer* and *The Jewish Bulletin* gave active support.

In estimating the value of the Congress, the question that has to be asked, as it must be asked of the subsequent life of the World Congress of Faiths, is whether, however worthy, the aims are sufficiently precise. The question of the relation to each other of the world religions is still much debated. The position of the Congress ruled out the view that any one religion had a monopoly of truth, assuming that, despite differences, the world religions have an affinity and share a recognition of spiritual reality and ethical values. It is therefore hardly surprising that many adherents of missionary religions opposed the Congress. On the other hand, the Congress ruled out the attempt to create a new synthetic religion, insisting that differences are important and must be respected. It was therefore criticized both by those who advocated a new unified religion and by those who held that differences are only external and irrelevant.

Is, then, the promotion of a spirit of fellowship and world loyalty a sufficient aim to engender enthusiasm? Clearly it has been for some, but the number of people, even including religious leaders, with a world consciousness and interest, has been small. How fellowship is understood may vary considerably. It should imply learning to appreciate others whose values and ways of life are different. In a world of prejudice, this is important, but somewhat negative. Fellowship may be concerned with the discovery of areas of ethical agreement and perhaps with taking common action on certain moral issues.

At its deepest level, the search for fellowship becomes a search for truth and flows from communion with the divine. Here it is assumed that the truth is greater than the understanding of any individual or of any one religion and that by sharing together with members of other faiths, each individual will be deepened in knowledge of truth and usually in appreciation of a personal religious tradition. It seems that Sir Francis Younghusband saw the development of all these aspects of fellowship as part of the work of the Congress, although he was aware of the difficulty of conveying exactly what he meant by fellowship. He perhaps came nearest to expressing his understanding in a talk given soon after the outbreak of war:

When I speak of fellowship I have found subtler and deeper meanings emerge as I study the idea more closely. It is not exactly either friendship, or companionship, or neighbourliness, or co-operation, though these may develop from it. And the sentiment from which it springs is something more than compassion, for compassion concerns itself with unhappiness alone rather than with both happiness and unhappiness. Even sympathy is associated rather with suffering than with enjoyment. At its intensest and highest, fellowship seems to be a communion of spirit greater, deeper, higher, wider, more universal, more fundamental than any of these – than even love.[18]

# 4. Hoping for a new world order in the midst of war: 1936–42

With the Congress drawing to its close, Younghusband wasted no time in thinking about the future. On the last day of the Congress, a meeting was held at Caxton Hall to consider what should happen next. The main suggestions were the formation of a continuation committee and the establishment of a council. Within a week, the continuation committee was meeting, with Dr Radhakrishnan, H. N. Spalding and Herbert Samuel amongst its members. Younghusband was at once elected chairman and Arthur Jackman secretary.

The chairman suggested that the next Congress might be in Oxford. He thought that many distinguished people from overseas would be in Britain for the Coronation. It was hoped the Congress would be held a week after the Coronation, which was planned for 12 May. It was not until 12 December 1936 that George VI was officially proclaimed King, following the abdication of Edward VIII.

It was also agreed to send a letter to Weller and Das Gupta 'explaining that while recognising our debt to them in carrying on the idea of the World Fellowship of Faiths, we must ask them to leave us perfectly free to pursue the outcome of the Congress and its subsequent work in our own way and in accordance with British practice'.

The name World Congress of Faiths was approved for the time being. Quite a lot of time was spent discussing an ultimately abortive scheme to show religious films followed by a short devotional service, conducted by members of different religions, in some cinemas on Sundays. Attention was also given to publishing the proceedings of the 1936 Congress and to agreeing a constitution and a publicity leaflet. Discussions were also initiated with some university extra-mural departments.

Early in 1937, Younghusband visited India to attend the centenary celebrations of the birth of Sri Ramakrishna, one of the outstanding Hindu saints of the nineteenth century, after whom the Ramakrishna Vedanta Society is named. His conference name badge survives amongst his papers. In the summer, the Oxford

Congress was held at Balliol and Somerville Colleges on the theme 'The World's Need of Religion'. The fact that it was residential made for greater discussion and fellowship.[1] The following year the Congress was held in Cambridge.[2]

The records of each Congress are of interest, partly to see the names of participants and partly because of the content of the talks and discussions. There is obviously not space to summarize all the conferences and this would be repetitive. It seems best to sample just a few of the early congresses and conferences. It is worth mentioning that there was talk of arranging a congress in Travancore and also in Beirut, before the committee settled on Paris. This indicates just how worldwide Younghusband hoped the WCF would become. He would have had the contacts to achieve this; world war was to thwart his hopes. The Paris conference itself was held less than two months before the outbreak of the Second World War.

## The Paris conference

The Paris conference was held at the Sorbonne from 3 to 11 July 1939 with some support from the French government. The theme was 'How to Promote the Spirit of World Fellowship through Religion'.

The conference attracted some eminent scholars. The most substantial paper – and certainly the most lengthy – was from the Catholic scholar Louis Massignon, who was a student of the works of St Thomas Aquinas, on whose writings classical Catholic thought has been based. Massignon began by observing that 'nothing in history goes to show that religious feeling or religious ideas have been particularly successful in pacifying men'. He stressed the need for people to be faithful to the light shown to them. He outlined the Catholic understanding of the relationship of religions. The doctrine that there is no salvation outside the Church 'means that there is no salvation outside the truth – which explicitly or implicitly and gratuitously offers itself to all'. The truth speaks to every human heart, wherever and whenever people may have lived. The fellowship WCF hoped to create was not at the level of intellectual agreement, but of love and friendship.

'In the first part', he eventually concluded, 'I emphasised the fundamental plurality of our respective points of view' but he had also spoken 'of a fellowship, based on friendship and leading to common action'.[3]

Baron Palmstierna, in the chair, tried to clarify the nature and purpose of the World Congress of Faiths:

> This is not a theological movement; it is not a movement for a comparative study of religions. It is a movement for really practical ends, a movement to create fellowship between men on the basis of that essence of religion that is common to all, which resides within all religions.[4]

## The outbreak of war

Even as war broke out, Younghusband and others were planning a conference which they hoped to hold in The Hague in 1940.[5] War was soon to change the way WCF worked. At the 1939 annual meeting, it was admitted that perhaps WCF should close down during the war as it was hard to promote fellowship amongst people who were bombing each other. Younghusband insisted that the need for WCF would be greater than ever when the war was over. 'By 2036', he said, 'we may be holding our centenary celebrations in a Europe where war is unthinkable.'[6] Throughout the war, a programme of meetings and conferences was maintained. Indeed, in the autumn of 1939, a series of monthly meetings was held in the office, now at Abbey House in Victoria Street. One meeting took place whilst an air raid was in progress.[7] The difficulties of travel, however, led Younghusband to start a chairman's letter to keep in touch with members.

Even war did not dent Younghusband's optimism. Indeed, almost at the beginning of the first chairman's circular letter, he wrote:

> Now in fact is our great opportunity. Now is when we are most needed. Lord Halifax spoke of building an international order based on mutual understanding and mutual confidence. And on the day of National Prayer the King and his people prayed that the nations of the world might be united in a firmer fellowship for the good of all mankind. Now you will

remember that to create that firmer fellowship between nations and individuals has been our one great object from the very first. Here we are, an organisation already in being designed especially to carry out the precise object which our Government have in distant view.[8]

## A new world order

The hope for a new world order is a recurrent theme. In the third chairman's letter, referring to youth being disillusioned with religion, Younghusband stressed the need for Christians and non-Christians together to show the value of religion. A religious basis, he insisted, was essential for the new world order. 'No reconstituted League of Nations', he had said earlier, 'will be of the slightest avail unless it is inspired by an irresistible spiritual impulse.'[9] He referred to the efforts of Rudolf Otto, best known for his book *The Idea of the Holy*, to create an inter-religious league as a parallel to the League of Nations. Not knowing much about this, Younghusband invited Rabbi Salzberger, who had known Otto, to speak to the members' meeting in April. A subsequent letter refers to a book by Professor Norman Bentwich, called *The Religious Foundation of Internationalism*, in which Bentwich expounded in detail the idea of a league of religions.[10] At a subsequent meeting, Bentwich said the idea had a long history: Leibnitz had propounded it and so had Rousseau. Incidentally Norman Bentwich maintained an interest in WCF, as did his brother, Joseph Bentwich, who settled in Israel. I met him there in the seventies and he introduced me to a small group concerned for inter-religious understanding, which produced a newsletter called *Petahim*.

Unable to meet in The Hague, the 1940 conference was held at Bedford College, London. Its theme was 'The Common Spiritual Basis for International Order'. Speakers included Lord Samuel, Bishop Bell of Chichester, Yusuf Ali, and Chief Rabbi Dr Hertz. The latter expressed 'his deep conviction that without a common spiritual basis for International Order we shall all be labouring in vain'. Lord Zetland, a member of the government, presided at the inaugural meeting and stressed the need for 'a spirit of religious unity'.[11]

The *Church Times* was not impressed. It 'suspected that the consequences of its [WCF's] labours are for the most part entirely mischievous . . . The results from such perverse efforts could only be to abolish the religion of God.'[12] Younghusband responded that for most people to listen to inspiring thinkers from each religion led them 'to a greater concept of God and what he wills for the world'.[13]

In the eleventh letter, Younghusband came back to the idea of a new world order, which was by then a subject of public discussion. He stressed that Christians should work with members of other faiths for this. He quoted from a *Times* leader that 'the fundamental precepts of Christianity are shared by millions in other lands and of other religions'. He also quoted words from the French philosopher Henri Bergson: 'God common to all mankind, the mere vision of Whom, could all men but attain it, would mean the immediate abolition of war'.[14]

The subject of the 1941 conference at Lady Margaret Hall, Oxford, was 'World Religions and World Order; the Interdependence of Religion and the Political, Economic, Social and Cultural aspects of the New World Order'. Younghusband was pleased with this sixth annual conference and Lord Samuel commented on the improvement in the quality of the contributions and the discussion. Addresses were given by, amongst others, Canon Grensted, the Regius Professor of Divinity at Oxford, and by Dr Gilbert Murray. Participants were invited to a service at the University Church.[15]

A smaller conference was also held in the spring of that year at Downe House, near Newbury. At this one of the speakers was Dr Maxwell Garnett, a former secretary of the League of Nations. At the closing session, Younghusband drew attention to a recent pronouncement made by Christian leaders and suggested that a similar pronouncement should be made by leaders of all the great religions. He returned to this theme at the annual meeting on 3 December 1941 and appealed to the Indian sage Sri Aurobindo to give a lead. Reference was also made to a suggestion by Sir James Marchant that there should be an international and inter-religious day of prayer.

It was natural for WCF to welcome the Atlantic Charter and, subsequently, the Three Faith Declaration. The Atlantic Charter was issued by Winston Churchill and President Roosevelt in August 1941 – the USA had not at that point entered the war. It was subsequently incorporated by reference in the Declaration of the United Nations (as the allied powers called themselves) of 1 January 1942. The Declaration affirmed that neither country sought territorial aggrandizement and described the just and peaceful world and settled economic order for which they hoped. The spring meeting of 1942, held at a much bomb-damaged Bedford College in London, was on 'The Atlantic Charter: Its Spiritual Basis'. Younghusband suggested that the influence of mothers was probably more important than that of popes and archbishops. The devotional service at the conference was led by Oliver Mathews, a priest of the Christian Community, a small denomination founded in Germany in the 1920s by some Lutheran priests, much influenced by Rudolf Steiner.

## Birmingham 1942

The summer conference was held at Birmingham on 'Religion Today: The Mutual Influence of East and West'. Some of the WCF officials thought it would be better to abandon plans for the conference. But when the office manager voiced this, Younghusband reacted swiftly. 'Miss Anderson,' he wrote, 'you, I know have the interests of the Congress most deeply at heart and I shall be ever grateful to you for the help you have given us for a long time past. But . . . ' She was dismissed and Sir Francis, now in his late seventies, personally took on the day-to-day running of the office.[16] Despite constant setbacks, he worked very hard to ensure the meeting's success. He and Lady Madeline Lees, whom he had first met in 1939 and with whom he formed an intimate friendship, stayed just outside the city with Dame Elizabeth Cadbury.

On 17 July Younghusband gave the opening address. He said that the need in the thirties had been for a Gladstone, with his passionate indignation, to denounce the Nazis. Sir Francis blamed himself for not creating WCF twelve years earlier. He came back to a theme that recurs in his later talks, namely the crucial role women should take in creating a more peaceful world. He insisted that when peace came there should be no vengeance, otherwise more conflict would follow in the future. Whilst repeating that WCF respected differences, he spoke of the need to stress the unity. This would make possible 'deep down genuine spiritual fellowship which would issue in the bliss divine of union with God, which is both the source and end of all religion, to which goal WCF presses forward'.[17]

The attendance was thin, but the atmosphere, he felt, was more inspired than ever. Speakers included Rabbi Georg Salzberger, Canon Guy Rogers and Swami Avyaktananda, whom I would later get to know when I lived in Bath.

It was on the fourth day, after listening to the last-named speaker, that Younghusband complained of feeling rather tired and was taken by taxi back to Dame Elizabeth's house. The next day he travelled by train to London to say goodbye to his wife, Helen. Before leaving Helen's nursing home, he wrote in a shaky hand to his daughter Eileen: 'My dear Rogie, the Congress was a huge success. The University, the Lord Mayor and Canon Guy Rogers all played up like Billy oh, and Sir Francis Younghusband . . . was a bit played out at the end so Madeline is motoring him straight to Lytchett today and he is giving the Men of the Trees the go by. Your loving Daddie.'[18]

Madeline managed to get him to her home in Dorset on 21 July. During the next few days, Younghusband slipped in and out of consciousness. Early in the morning of Friday 31 July 1942, he died calmly and peacefully, cradled in the arms of Lady Madeline Lees.

He was buried nearby. Tributes poured in from around the world. On 10 August, WCF arranged a memorial service for him at St Martin-in-the-Fields. Speakers included many of his faithful allies: Bhikkhu Thittila, Sir Atul Chatterjee, Rabbi Dr Salzberger and Sir Hassan Suhrawardy. It was fitting that he who had done so much in his life to bring people of different faiths together in fellowship should also have united them in mourning for him.

# 5. Carrying on: 1942–52

Younghusband concentrated all the work of WCF in his own hands, as Baron Palmstierna observed in the first circular to be sent out after Sir Francis's death. This was appropriate for a pioneer, Palmstierna added, but his successors would have to rely on teamwork. Lord Samuel became chairman of the executive committee, and Baron Erik Palmstierna chairman of the action committee, while Lady Ravensdale took on responsibility as treasurer and chairman of the finance committee.

Herbert Samuel, who was created a viscount in 1937, was one of the first Jewish members of the British cabinet. He was a member of Campbell-Bannerman's Liberal government. In 1916, for a few months, he was Home Secretary and again in 1931. From 1920 to 1925, he was British High Commissioner for Palestine. After the Second World War, he became leader of the Liberals in the House of Lords. He wrote a number of books, including *Philosophy and the Ordinary Man*, *The Tree of Good and Evil* and *Belief and Action*. Herbert Samuel showed a consistent interest in WCF and was a man of wide contacts and sound judgement.

Baron Palmstierna had been for a short while Foreign Minister of Sweden and then from 1920 to 1937 he was Swedish ambassador to Britain. When he retired from diplomatic service, he stayed on in Britain, finding a kindred spirit in Younghusband. He was an effusive and spontaneous man and a good extempore speaker. His books, *Widening Horizons*, *Horizons of Immortality* and *The Innocence of God* reflect his deep spiritual interests.

Lady Ravensdale was the daughter of Lord Curzon, the Viceroy of India who appointed Younghusband to lead the expedition to Tibet. She was well known for her love of music and for her social welfare work, especially in the East End of London. She was intimately involved in the foundation of WCF from 1936 onwards and continued to work for what she called a 'spiritual design for living in a greater universalism'. A devout Anglican, it was she who introduced W. W. Matthews, the Dean of St Paul's Cathedral, and Dr Edward Carpenter to WCF. She had a considerable knowledge of eastern religions and wrote movingly of a pilgrimage to Benares.

L to R: Lord Samuel, Bishop Bell, Rabbi Isaac Livingstone and the head of the Buddhist Vihara [E. H. Emanuel – Courtesy *The Jewish Chronicle*]

'Hindu worship', wrote Heather McConnell of her after her death, 'struck her as a great irresistibly pulsing heartbeat offered to the Eternal Unknown. Visits to Sri Lanka and Burma, where in Rangoon, she barefoot joined the pilgrims climbing the hundreds of steps up the Shwedagon Pagoda, added to her feeling that some part of her being was only completely fulfilled in the East.'[1] She continued throughout her life to be a generous and loyal supporter of the Congress and made possible the purchase of Younghusband House.

Arthur Jackman was appointed honorary secretary. Five new members joined the executive: Eileen Younghusband, Sir Francis's daughter, Sir John Stewart-Wallace, who was Chief Land Registrar for England and Wales from 1923 to 1944, Paul Shuffrey, editor of the *Guardian*, the Revd W. W. Simpson, at the time secretary to the Christian Council for Refugees from Germany, who was soon to become secretary of the Council of Christians and Jews, and the Revd J. van Dorp, rector of the Dutch Church in London. It is noticeable that the majority of members of the executive were British and Christian. Steps were taken to register the movement as a legal entity.

Palmstierna wrote the first circular letter of 1943. When this was replaced by the journal *Forum*, he continued until his death to contribute a letter to each issue. In the first circular letter, Palmstierna paid tribute to Sir Francis and insisted that the work must be carried on: 'Lasting peace and progressive order cannot be reached on earth until the spirit of fellowship quickens in human souls and mankind realises that all spring from the same source of Life and Love.' He indicated that it had been agreed to hold a big public meeting in May and that plans were in hand to continue the series of annual conferences.[2]

Palmstierna's next letter tells of further activity. The Brotherhood Movement had become affiliated to WCF, a library was being created, members' meetings were being held regularly and the public meeting had been fixed for 4 June 1943, with R. A. Butler, president of the Board of Education, as one of the speakers. An annual conference was to be held in London in September on 'The Religions and World Recovery'. The office had been moved to Parliament Mansions in Abbey Orchard Street.

## A public meeting

Because Caxton Hall had been requisitioned, the public meeting was held in Central Hall, Westminster, where an audience of 750 people looked rather lost. The chair was taken by Lord Samuel, who outlined the action that had been taken since Younghusband's death. He also reiterated the purpose for which WCF existed. He again rejected the idea 'which prevails in some quarters that the object of WCF is to create some new combined religion':

Each member holds his own views and holds them tenaciously. This Movement does not enter into any of those disputations, it merely declares that all religions worthy of the name have at least two common principles, one that they seek righteous conduct in the individual, the other that they inculcate good-will among human societies, each with its own particularities and so each has its own element of universalism. This last I wish to stress, this element of universalism and we wish to bring it out clearly before members of all Faiths.[3]

The main address was given by R. A. Butler, who after some years as under-secretary in the India Office and the Foreign Office had become Minister of Education. Religious education and worship in schools continues to be a subject of keen debate. In view of the influential 1944 Education Act, with its important sections on religious instruction and collective worship, Butler's talk is of particular interest. He suggested that despite significant differences between creeds, what is 'of transcendent value is common to us all – the fact of faith'. He quoted a poet:

> Think not the faith by which the just shall live
> Is a dead creed, a map correct of heaven,
> Far less a feeling fond and fugitive,
> A thoughtless gift withdrawn as soon as given;
> It is an affirmation and an act
> Which makes eternal truth be present fact.

Butler stressed the importance of faith in helping the United Nations to resist Nazism. The personal values of our civilization, he said, depended mainly upon the development of the spiritual life. His first point was 'that these spiritual values are emphasised in all the Faiths of the world and not only in Christianity'. Religious education had been a cause of much controversy, with complaints being made that schools were godless. He was awaiting evidence from school inspectors, but certainly felt that arrangements were too haphazard. He went on:

> I can tell you that it is the Government's intention that religious teaching shall take a definite, enduring and assured place in the school day. It is our intention that all children shall be given the opportunity of being brought up in the faith of their parents. The rights of conscience must remain inviolate and distinctive teaching must be available where desired for children by parents. I have discussed this with the Chief Rabbi and others.

The broad foundations of religious teaching were already present in the agreed syllabuses: 'These are not intended to be a form of State religion but are the beginnings of the teaching in what I may call the literacy of faith.' Butler's hope was that, in addition, for those who desired, there would be teaching on special faiths. He warned against the harmful effect of dissension amongst Church leaders on the subject.[4]

The Dean of St Paul's, W. W. Matthews, made clear that he was a convinced Christian and that he rejected the idea of a pale abstraction from all religions. He stressed the importance of understanding others at their best and that members of one faith can learn from members of another faith.

## The 1943 conference

The next letter, which appeared in the spring of 1944, mentions the 1943 conference, which was held at the Institut Français. It explains that plans for a congress in Edinburgh had to be abandoned. Members' meetings were continuing, but clearly the strains of wartime conditions were making it difficult to maintain the momentum of the congress. Ill health had led Lord Samuel to resign as chairman of the executive and his place had been taken by Baron Palmstierna.

## The Three Faith Declaration

The most interesting activity at the time was WCF's effort to canvass support for the Three Faith Declaration on World Peace. It is reminiscent of recent attempts, following the 1993 Parliament of the World's Religions, to gain support for the Declaration Toward a Global Ethic.

On 4 April 1943, Dr George Bell, the Bishop of Chichester, spoke in the House of Lords of 'the acceptance of an absolute law with a common ethos to be secured in the dealings of nations with each other' and 'of an association between the International Authority and representatives of the living religions of the world'.[5] The Bishop was subsequently invited to submit his proposal to the executive of WCF. In a letter dated 17 April 1943, recognizing that the League of Nations lacked a supporting religious body, he wrote: 'my idea was whether there could be some group officially recognized of representatives of all religions' – an idea which has resurfaced fifty years later with talk of a World Council of Faiths or a United Religions Organization.

The WCF executive asked Dr Bell to set up a private committee to examine the proposal in detail and to report back. The committee included Lord Perth, late Secretary-General of the League of Nations, Lord Samuel, Sir S. Runganadhan, Indian High Commissioner, Baron Palmstierna and M. Mo'een al-Arab, secretary of the Royal Egyptian Embassy in London. After several meetings it was unanimously agreed to ask WCF to circulate the Three Faith Declaration on World Peace.

The American Three Faith Declaration had been issued in October 1943 over some 140 signatures of authoritative leaders of the Protestant, Catholic and Jewish communities. The Declaration proclaimed:

1. that the moral law must govern the world order;
2. that the rights of the individual must be assured;
3. that the rights of the oppressed, weak or coloured [sic] peoples must be protected;
4. that the rights of minorities must be secured;
5. that international institutions to maintain peace with justice must be organized;
6. that international economic co-operation must be developed;
7. that a just social order within each state must be achieved.

In Britain, the statement gained the support of the Council of Christians and Jews. CCJ's executive issued a statement affirming that 'there can be no permanent peace without a religious foundation'. All social righteousness had to rest on divine law:

The re-establishment of moral law, of respect for the rights of the person, especially those of the poor, the weak and the backward, and of responsibility towards the whole community, must be the first charges on the energies of all right-thinking men and women.[6]

The Bishop of Chichester's committee invited WCF to make the Declaration and Statement known to religious leaders of the world and to enlist their support. This was done through embassies, legations and rectors of foreign Churches in London. By mid 1946, 1,050 copies had been despatched. Several copies sent to European countries were returned by the censor. WCF kept Dr Lois Finkelstein of the Jewish Theological Seminary of the USA, one of the original signatories, informed of the response.

Pamphlet 27 of 1946 shows an interesting range of supporters, including the Sheikh of the mosque at Mecca, as well as Muslim leaders from Iraq and Syria. The Dewan of Travancore affirmed his sympathy as did the Raja of Aundh. The Sadharan Brahmo Samaj published the document in full in its newsletter. The Archbishop of Sweden, after consultation with the Swedish Ecumenic Committee, expressed his whole-hearted agreement. To Palmstierna's bitter disappointment, however, there was little backing for the initiative from most Christian leaders. In any case, the Communist bloc prevented the United Nations from any public endorsement of religious principles. A reception was arranged for members of UN delegations during the first meeting of the assembly in London in 1946 to tell them about the Declaration, but only a few people turned up.

WCF had done all it could, but religious leaders failed to build on this initiative. I hope that fifty years later the same will not be true of the Declaration Toward a Global Ethic.

## 1945–50

Apart from work on the Three Faith Declaration, the next period shows no enormous sign of activity. There were a few members' meetings. Arthur Jackman had resigned – the minutes make clear that he and Palmstierna could not work together.[7] An honorary secretary was appointed *pro tem* but this was not a success. 'For a few brief months the chairman and Hon. treasurer [Lady Ravensdale] were assisted by a "pro tem" Hon. Secretary – a renegade whose name had better not be mentioned, for there was more "pro tem" about him than any right to the title,' said Baron Palmstierna in his annual report for 1945. To my disappointment, none of the minute books reveal the secretary's name and *pro tem* has to become synonymous with *anon*.[8]

By early 1946, Sir John Stewart-Wallace had become honorary secretary. The Congress also had various office secretaries, sometimes part time, sometimes full time. By late 1945, a new secretary, Iris Wade, who commuted from Brighton, had been appointed. Her salary was £250 per annum, plus the cost of a third-class season ticket from Brighton, which was then £10. I doubt whether you would now get a day ticket for that amount!

It is easy to underestimate the difficulties of life in Britain in the years immediately after the war, but the impression given by the various changes of staff is that no one of Arthur Jackman's experience and ability was available to take on the running of the organization and that this was the point at which WCF lost much of the momentum created by Younghusband.

The next circular letter I have come across is No. 3, 1948, dated October. Minutes for the intervening years do not show much activity. At the annual meeting on 19 February 1948, the executive committee was forced to recommend that, because of lack of money and decreasing support, the movement should go into 'cold storage' until such time as conditions improved. In the ensuing discussion, 'it was clear that the members were vigorously against the closing-down of the Movement and many pledged their support to help keep it going'.[9]

It was left to the executive to take appropriate action. For a time the office was closed and moved to the country under the directorship of Colonel van Dorp. This proved to be a failure, even before Colonel van Dorp's death made other plans essential. Lady Ravensdale appealed to Sir John Stewart-Wallace to take over the reorganization of the society and to reopen a London office. He agreed to do so. A restatement of the purposes of the Congress was produced. Heather McConnell started to edit a magazine called *Forum*, which replaced the chairman's letter. A youth group was set up, again thanks to the energy of Heather McConnell. A series of meetings on contemplative meditation was arranged, led by the Revd R. G. Coulson. His son-in-law, Viscount Combermere, was to become chairman of WCF in the eighties.

R. G. Coulson, in his book *I Am*, explained the purpose of the contemplative meetings. Previously, in his view, WCF had confined itself to 'exercises in comparative religion which led to increased sympathy between the great institutions. But little actual co-operation followed, and certainly little real prospect emerged of a united search for the I AM, as the Lord of The All.'[10] Agreeing to put aside dogmatic differences, some Christians, Hindus and Buddhists were prepared to come together for a joint experience in contemplative silence. A single meeting enabled them to reach a truly joint experience of the Supreme. Slowly they found that they agreed that 'the Supreme is the entire Reality composed of three essential aspects which are indissolubly interrelated'. The first aspect of the Supreme is the Nameless, the second aspect is the Infinite manifested as knowable and the third aspect is 'actually made known on this earth as incarnate in particular corporeal Selves'.[11]

This experiment in the early fifties is of considerable interest. Sadly, there was soon disagreement between Coulson and Stewart-Wallace, as surviving letters indicate. Coulson insisted that only committed members of a faith should be invited to these meditation meetings. Stewart-Wallace wanted 'seekers' to be invited and seems to have seen WCF as a new spiritual movement.

Sir John Stewart-Wallace was critical of traditional orthodox religions. The high religion of the future of which he wrote would be for those who could no longer accept traditional doctrines. It would be universal in character. 'Only through a high religion, all-embracing and tolerant as the love of God, can mankind be linked in the bond of peace for which the whole world so piteously travaileth – and for which, without religion, the politicians travail in vain.'[12] In an article in *The Hibbert Journal*, Sir John asked why

any suggestion of synthesis in religion is anathema to the orthodox . . . The great cosmic process is confused with an attempt to make some superficial, eclectic religion . . . Behind and above all the World Faiths there is to-day, here and now, a transcendent *oneness*, a Fellowship of the Spirit, of which the world, breaking from the swaddling clothes of the institutional theologies, is becoming conscious . . . At the heart of the synthesis lies the ever-living spring of all religion . . . the mystic vision.[13]

Under Stewart-Wallace's guidance, it is clear that the Congress had regained some of its lost vigour. The emphasis, however, had subtly changed. The new leaflet talked of two categories of members: those who were committed members of a faith and those who were 'seekers'. The latter were people interested in spiritual matters, but who were unable to accept the tenets of any particular faith and who did not belong to any particular faith community. Seekers have continued to be welcome members of WCF, but if they appear to be in the majority they may deter committed members of faith communities from joining, as they may be uneasy with what they feel is the unspoken assumption that all religions 'really say the same thing'. The introduction of sessions on contemplative meditation may have added spiritual depth, but may have reinforced the impression that the Congress was a private spiritual group. There was perhaps also more emphasis on the underlying unity of religions. Religion, in Object One, is 'interpreted in its wide and universal sense. A sense far transcending its particular expression in any one of the world's faiths and penetrating to that divine essence we believe to be common to them all.'[14]

Younghusband himself no doubt believed this, but was always more cautious about voicing this in public, and the claim was certainly not so 'up front' in earlier leaflets. Any idea of a new amalgamated creed is rejected, but there is less about the differences between religions. This was at a time when the mood in the Churches had become less sympathetic to other religions, under the impact of Hendrik Kraemer, a Protestant missionary theologian who in 1938 wrote a very influential book called *The Christian Message in a Non-Christian World*, which sharply distinguished between the religions and the Gospel.[15]

A series of lectures on 'The Drama of Faith and Belief', held at Caxton Hall to coincide with the Festival of Britain, was poorly attended. The lack of big public meetings lessened the emphasis on world concerns and may have further reinforced the feeling that WCF was in danger of becoming a spiritual coterie, despite the universalism of its message. Indeed, in a circular, Baron Palmstierna said he thought the time for big congresses was over.

There were some continuing international links, but Younghusband's sense that WCF was an international movement had receded. Baron Palmstierna, in a newsletter, mentioned that he and Sir John had attended a conference in Paris arranged by the World Alliance for International Friendship through Religion (USA). For a time WCF received some financial help from this body. A leaflet from this period describes a conference in Paris arranged by French members of the Congress. The French *Union des Croyants* was quite active and had the support of Teilhard de Chardin. The Paris conference was attended by representatives of the British, French, Dutch and Indian branches. It was agreed to set up an international central committee, but it seems that little came of this.

WCF had avoided 'going into cold storage', but the theological mood of the Churches was now unsympathetic to its aims. The Empire and British interest in it and its religions had waned. As yet, Britain had not in a significant sense begun to become a multiracial and multifaith society. The Cold War had dashed hopes of building a new moral world order. Nonetheless, a few people kept alive the original vision of the World Congress of Faiths for a time when its importance was again to be more widely recognized.

# 6. New shoots: 1952–67

India gained its independence in 1947. An even more important date, however, in marking the end of British imperial ambition is Sir Anthony Eden's disastrous attempt to seize the Suez Canal in 1956. By the late fifties, the Empire was being metamorphosed into the Commonwealth. On a visit to South Africa, Harold Macmillan spoke of winds of change. Those who had served the Empire were growing older and this meant that the appeal of the World Congress of Faiths began to alter.

At the same time as Britain was adjusting to a new role in the world, so British society was changing. After the Second World War some Midland firms recruited labour in the Indian subcontinent. Immigrants also came to Britain from the West Indies. By the early sixties, restrictions were being imposed on the number of immigrants allowed into Britain. Nonetheless, Britain was starting to become a multiracial and multireligious society, although, as now, the ethnic minorities were concentrated in the major conurbations.

Slowly the media began to notice the change. In 1954, the Home Service of the BBC broadcast a series of talks about the religions of the world. Canon Charles Raven, an active member of WCF, wrote an introductory article in the *Radio Times*. An article in *The Christian* in October 1957 referred to the presence in Britain of immigrants and students who belonged to other faiths. In 1959, *Good Cookery* had a series of articles about the religions of the world. The next year *The Times*, not to be outdone, had an interesting article about eastern religions establishing themselves in Britain: 'A remarkable array of oriental religions can be found – and found to be flourishing today – in Britain.' The article referred to the Woking Mosque, to Shanti Sadan in Notting Hill Gate, to Swami Avyaktananda's centre in Bath, to the Sikh Gurdwara in Shepherd's Bush and to Zoroastrian House, which had recently been opened. 'Between them and the Jewish communities, the World Congress of Faiths has helped to maintain a deal of good will.'[1]

Yet there was a general lack of interest in other faiths. In 1961, the BBC refused Lady Ravensdale's offer to endow a series of broadcast lectures about the great faiths. As late as 1980,

Clifford Longley, religious affairs correspondent for *The Times*, could say that 'the main denominations know far more about each other than they do about non-Christian religions, and tend to treat those outside any formal belief system as mere "tabula rasa" needing not understanding but conversion "from scratch"'. He noted Archbishop Runcie's wish to talk to and learn from people of other faiths as a new departure which 'for reasons of inherited prejudice, the Church of England and the Free Churches have shied away from'.[2] This is why Dr Runcie's 1986 Younghusband Lecture was so important, not only for what he said but for its symbolic significance, although admittedly the series of Lambeth Interfaith Lectures was started under his predecessor, Dr Donald Coggan. It was only in 1977 that the British Council of Churches established its Committee for Relations with People of Other Faiths.

The widespread British indifference to the understanding of other religions, except amongst orientalists and some missionaries, may be illustrated by the situation at Cambridge University, when I was an undergraduate in the early sixties. The Revd Dr A. C. Bouquet, who had a few years before published *Comparative Religion* and *Sacred Books of the World*, gave the only lectures on the subject. They were held in the May term, which was dominated by examinations, at 5.00 in the afternoon, when no one in the summer expected to be indoors. It was assumed that hardly anyone would come and the assumption was self-fulfilling. Before I went to Madras Christian College, Dr Bouquet invited me to tea and gave me much helpful advice about India. He saw Christianity as fulfilling all that was best in other faiths. The frontispiece of his *Sacred Books of the World* has two quotations from Justin Martyr. It will suffice to quote one: 'We have shown that Christ is the Word [*Logos*] of whom the whole human race are partakers, and those who lived according to reason [*logos*] are Christians, even though accounted atheists.'[3]

A letter from Dr Bouquet to Bishop Bell of Chichester, written in 1956, casts an interesting light on how WCF was perceived at the time. The suggestion had been made that the Cambridge Society for the Study of Religion should become in effect the Cambridge University branch of the World Congress of Faiths. Bouquet was concerned about this, as in 1951 he had joined the WCF council, but quickly felt himself compromised as an Anglican clergyman – evidence of the mood under Sir John Stewart-Wallace's leadership. Bouquet had noticed, however, that Bishop Bell had taken part in the dedication of Younghusband House. Bell, in his reply, said that WCF had changed and referred Bouquet to Lord Samuel's statement, which is quoted below, on the occasion of the opening of Younghusband House.

Despite Dr Bouquet, Canon Raven, Dr W. W. Matthews and one or two more clergy, Christian thinking about other religions was still negative. It was dominated by the influence of Karl Barth and Hendrik Kraemer, who, as has been mentioned, stressed the discontinuity between the Gospel and the religions of the world.

By the early sixties, a few Church leaders were giving attention to the new situation. Max Warren, an experienced missionary, wrote: 'The Christian Church has not yet seriously faced the theological problems of "co-existence" with other religions.'[4] This was in the introduction to an influential series of books called 'The Christian Presence'. Contributors, including George Appleton and Kenneth Cragg, wrote in a sympathetic way about other religions.

In a sermon preached about this time for the World Congress of Faiths at St Paul's Cathedral, Dean Matthews elaborated on his understanding of the work of WCF. He outlined five points:

1. Members of WCF believe that religion is the most important thing in the world and that there is an urgent need to bring all the indifferent people who are untouched by religion to see that this is so.
2. They recognize the multiplicity of religions.
3. They believe 'that the first step in a study of religions other than our own should be an attempt to understand and to try to grasp the meaning of each religion on its highest level, as experienced and explained by its saints and thinkers'.
4. They hope that the way of understanding may lead us to see that, at their best, the spiritual religions converge . . . and, if this is the case, there may well be some divine revelation in other religions from which we might profit ourselves. The Holy Spirit has been at work in them and we may gain some new insights and inspiration from them.

5. They are not trying to make a new religion from a mixture of all the religions of the world. Its members hold fast to their own faith, whatever that may be.

Turning then to his position as a Christian, Matthews did not question the missionary command, but thought more was achieved by appreciation of others than denunciation: 'We come not to destroy, but to fulfil.' By this means, he said, 'we shall be led to a deeper apprehension of our own religion'. Others ask: 'Is not your quest hopeless?' He agreed that profound differences between religions could not be overlooked: 'Any attempt to reconcile ideas of the Divine in Buddhism and Christianity appears to be hopeless.' Yet 'all the saints of all the religions agree that the Divine is not material and it is not unreasoning force or fate. They agree too, I would urge, in believing that we must seek for any suggestion of the nature of the Divine within the spirit of man.' There are agreements too in their view of humanity and on what makes for the true good of humankind.[5]

Other Anglican clergy who became supporters of WCF at this time included Edward Carpenter, a canon of Westminster Cathedral, who was to give increasing support to WCF and to become its president, and George Appleton, who was to become chairman. As vicar of St Botolph's Church in the City of London, Appleton invited WCF to hold its 1958 annual service there. This was, it appears, the first interfaith service to be held in an Anglican church.

## Younghusband House

For WCF, an important achievement was the purchase of Younghusband House, 23 Norfolk Square, near Paddington Station. It provided a spacious meeting room on the first floor, and offices for the honorary secretary. On the ground floor there was an office for the housekeeper and for the office secretary, and also a library and reading room. The cost of shelving and equipping the library was met by the Spalding Trust. The rest of the house consisted of furnished bed-sitting rooms and a furnished flat. The weekly charge for a single room, with breakfast, was £3. 5s 0d. The house was vested in the World Congress of Faiths Trustee

The Spalding Room with the library at Younghusband House [Owen Thomas]

Association Ltd, which has now been wound up. Its cost was £5,600, met by a loan from Lady Ravensdale. Members raised £1,700 towards the cost of furnishings and decoration.

The opening must have been an impressive occasion, with a talk by Lord Samuel and prayers offered by the Bishop of Chichester, by Rabbi Livingstone and by members of other faiths. The opening received fair coverage in the national press. Lord Samuel said it had been hoped that religious intolerance was fading but, sadly, religious antagonisms had again become a principal feature in world affairs. There were, he said, some 2,500 million members of religions in the world. Was it not common sense, as well as a duty, for them all to dispute less and to co-operate more? He mentioned that WCF was hampered by persistent misunderstanding of its purpose. People seemed to think the aim was to amalgamate religions:

That has never been the aim and it is not now. . . . The principle has been – I have my belief, you have yours – on that understanding let us work together to soften antagonisms, to organise co-operation; to bring the leaders of all faiths together in order to promote goodwill among their followers and so guide mankind along the ways of gentleness and the paths of peace.[6]

Unfortunately, the house was difficult to run and there were financial problems, accentuated by the discovery of dry rot. The first meeting that I attended at Younghusband House was in the gracious upstairs lecture room. The speaker was Professor Geoffrey Parrinder of King's College, London, who by both his teaching and writing did much to encourage a scholarly interest in the world's religions. By the time I next visited the house, WCF had retreated to the ground floor. In 1965, the house was sold to St Mary's Hospital, Paddington, to be a nurses' hostel, with the ground floor leased to WCF. The front room became the meeting room, with the adjoining room as the office. The Spalding Room remained the library.

In 1967, after Joan Dopping, who had been a conscientious and helpful librarian, resigned, most of the books were given to the Selly Oak Colleges. Others have now found a home at Westminster College, as part of the recently established International Interfaith Centre there. I regretted this, particularly as I had made considerable use of the library in writing a thesis for the London Master of Philosophy degree – material which I used in my book *Together to the Truth*. When I became executive director of the Council of Christians and Jews in the eighties, it too had just disposed of its library. Increasing postal costs made lending libraries less useful: but there were several books in the WCF library, published in India, which were not readily available anywhere else in Britain.

The eventual sale of the property made it possible to repay the loan and provided WCF with some capital. No one at the time knew how property prices were to soar in the seventies. WCF never seems to have been destined to be wealthy, but there is much in most religions about renunciation and the way of poverty!

When WCF's lease ran out, there was a further retreat, to save money, into the Spalding Room, until costs eventually forced WCF to move out of the house altogether – only the fanlight, painted with the bold letters 'YOUNGHUSBAND HOUSE', are a reminder of its former use.[7]

## Arthur Peacock

The moving spirit during the fifties was the Revd Arthur Peacock. Following the resignation as chairman of Sir John Stewart-Wallace because of illness, Lady Ravensdale combined the positions of treasurer and chairman. At the same time, Lord Samuel became president in place of Baron Palmstierna. It is clear that the main responsibility for running the Congress rested with Arthur Peacock who became honorary secretary in 1951.

As a young man, Arthur Peacock became editor of the *Clarion* and for fifteen years he was secretary of the National Trade Union Club. In 1937 he became a minister of the Universalist Church. This was quite a strong body in the USA, where the American Unitarian Association and the Universalist Church of America merged in 1961 to form the Unitarian Universalist Association. In Britain, the Universalist Church was always very small and gradually disappeared, with many of its members joining the Unitarian Church, as Peacock himself did. In 1951 he became a Unitarian minister. He did much to help build up the social service department of the Unitarian Church.

He was an imaginative and energetic secretary. He was, as an ex-journalist, a fluent writer and wrote *Fellowship through Religions*, which tells the history of the first twenty years of the Congress. His motto was a verse from Elizabeth Barrett Browning:

> Universalism – universe religion – the unity of all things,
> Why it's the greatest word in our language.[8]

Arthur Peacock left in 1959, 'under a cloud', but I have not been able to discover what the problem was. At executive committee meetings in 1961 there were heated debates about whether Peacock should still be invited to review books for the journal.

His place as secretary was taken by Fr Lev Gillet, an Orthodox priest with an amazing range of knowledge, shown in his extensive book reviews for the Spalding Trust newsletter.

An interesting memo survives of some suggestions that he made to the executive committee. He wanted university theological students to be made aware of and to use the library. He suggested a year-book to serve two purposes:

> 1. An objective account of the main events having happened during the year in all the great religions – not journalistic – try to show the trends of thought at work in these events;
> 2. An objective review – short, not articles – of the main books on the subject published during the year.

He also proposed a World Council of Religion, which is particularly interesting in view of the establishment in the eighties, thanks partly to the efforts of WCF, of an International Interfaith Organizations Co-ordinating Committee. At this time there was also talk about the need for a World Council of Religion. As we shall see when we look at WCF's international work, no such council has been established although the idea reappears from time to time. 'Implement this idea of Younghusband and Spalding', Lev Gillet wrote in his telegraphic style:

> The World Congress of Faiths cannot, of course, do this alone, but can provoke and stimulate. Try to form an initiative group or committee, not asking at the start Churches or Associations, etc, but well-known individuals – e.g. Buber, Suzuki, Kagawa, Vinobha Bhave, Radhakrishnan, Taha Hussein. Correspond with them actively. Find, with them, how to approach the 'collectivities'. This requires faith, intensity of feeling and will and firm decision not to drag on, but act quickly.

The first steps, he suggested, were to consult with Dr Heiler and Canon Raven. Fr Lev Gillet also suggested that prayer or meditation meetings should be held at Younghusband House for those who wished to attend.[9]

For a while Heather McConnell was joint honorary secretary with Fr Gillet, but in 1963 the Revd John Rowland, a Unitarian minister, combined this work with his position as treasurer. Another active worker for WCF at this time, especially in the north of England, was George Harrison, who was a great admirer of Younghusband. He was himself also of a mystical inclination.

In 1959, Lord Samuel resigned as president, because of age.

L to R: Lady Stansgate, Lady Ravensdale, the Hon. Mrs de Beaumont and Maung Maung Ji [Sabra]

His position was taken by Lady Ravensdale, who remained as president until her death on 9 February 1966. She was succeeded by Dr Edward Carpenter, who at the time was Archdeacon of Westminster and who became Dean. He had long been a supporter of the Congress and of a wide range of organizations concerned for peace and human rights. He and his wife, Lilian, both of whom have regularly attended WCF events, made the Deanery a home for all who were active in the interfaith movement. By their wisdom, wide contacts and personal charm they have made an incalculable contribution to the life of the Congress.

## Reg Sorensen

In 1959 the Revd Reginald Sorensen MP, who in 1964 was created a baron, became chairman and retained the office until his death in 1970. Born at Highbury, London, in 1891, Sorensen entered Parliament in 1929, by winning the seat of West Leyton for Labour. He was defeated in 1931, but in 1935 regained the seat, which he held until 1950. After boundary changes, he became MP for Leyton from 1950 to 1964, when he accepted a life peerage, in

Muriel and Reg Sorensen [Courtesy Guardian and Gazette Series]

the hope of enabling Gordon Walker, the Foreign Secretary, who had lost his own seat, to re-enter Parliament. In the event, in a sensational result, Gordon Walker was defeated by the Conservative candidate.

Reg Sorensen was a tireless worker for numerous causes. He was a convinced pacifist and was president of the International Friendship League and chairman of the National Peace Council. He was an admirer of Mahatma Gandhi and one of the first British politicians to advocate Indian independence. In 1958, he received the freedom of Leyton. I remember at his memorial service in the town hall the innumerable organizations that were represented and paid tribute to his work for them.

He and his wife, Muriel, brought to the World Congress of

Faiths their wide concerns and contacts, their gift of friendship and their kindness to individuals of all races and conditions. Reg was a Unitarian and his interest was especially in seeking the common moral values contained in the teachings of the world religions. The emphasis shifted, therefore, away from the mystical.

Conscious of the obscurantist and reactionary character of so much religion, Reg Sorensen had a love–hate relationship with organized religion. In his book *I Believe in Man*, he criticized religions' opposition to new knowledge, to scientific advance and to social progress. In a letter to Heather McConnell he said: 'I do *not* think the book is suitable for the WCF and would certainly not wish it to be displayed at WCF gatherings because it would be too challenging and provocative to many of our members.' He added a PS to his letter that he was sorry that Edward Carpenter had mentioned it at the annual service.[10]

Sorensen disliked all intolerance and found orthodox Christianity too rigid and dogmatic. Yet he never doubted that the human spirit could commune with the divine and sought to commend a 'modern faith': 'I affirm that we should not be seduced into thinking that the only reality is the tangible and the sensuous, but that reality is vaster and more permeative of our material environment than we can neatly tie up with intellectual string.'[11]

With his belief in a divine spirit went a deep and optimistic belief in the human spirit and in humankind's ability eventually to overcome evil and suffering in the world. He held that this belief was enshrined in all the great religious traditions and hoped that the Congress could help the religions emphasize the ethical values that they held in common. Impatient with doctrinal debate or theological dialogue – despite his questioning mind – again and again Reg Sorensen, in his addresses, came back to matters of ethical and moral concern.

He was well aware of the endless variations of moral patterns or 'mores', but held that there could be found in the world religions an essential moral content beyond transient communal codes. He said at a conference service:

> It is necessary to distinguish between paramount moral values and what I term 'moral patterns' . . . Moral patterns vary considerably, but penetrating, yet transcending those variables

are moral values, that, with degrees of priority and emphasis, exist within all faiths and religions. Among these are justice, mercy, compassion, integrity, courage, sacrifice, fidelity and fraternity. Here is where all can meet on common ground.

He believed that despite differences of metaphysics and custom, all religions could agree on these moral values and that such agreement was vital for the world: 'I would claim that only a measure of inter-religious, international and inter-racial agreement on essential moral values can enable mankind to dwell on this earth in co-operation, amity and peace.'[12]

Lord Sorensen was chairman when I became joint honorary secretary. He and his wife had a great gift of friendship. At annual conferences they would make a point of speaking to everyone. I have happy memories of their visit to our home in London and then in Kent, where Reg preached at a local interfaith service. He had a quizzical and enquiring mind and a great sense of fun, shown by his skill as a ventriloquist.

With his death, the dominant contribution that Unitarians had made to the leadership of WCF was to fade. Subsequent chairmen have all been members of the Church of England, although all would probably share Edward Carpenter's sentiment that they are grateful to the C of E, but glad to have spent a lot of their time outside it!

# 7. Keeping up with a changing world: 1967–96

For most of the period since 1966 I have been on the executive committee of WCF and for much of the time an officer, either as honorary secretary, editor of the journal or chairman. Throughout this time, the story has been sadly repetitive: a recurring problem of lack of money. Some fresh initiative which has increased activity and interest has created too much work for the over-burdened secretariat. The inability to raise significant funds may reflect a lack of clarity about the purposes and identity of the Congress.

Over the past thirty years there have been many changes of officers and repeated attempts to redefine WCF's role in a changing world. In July 1965, I was one of four people approached by Lord Sorensen to consider being put forward for the post of honorary secretary. The Revd John Rowland had resigned because he was moving to Kent, although he continued as honorary treasurer. Soon afterwards Fr Lev Gillet indicated his wish to resign. At the AGM early in 1966, the Revd Tom Dalton, a Unitarian minister in North London, and I were elected joint honorary secretaries. I soon became responsible for planning the annual service and annual conference whilst Tom Dalton looked after the business concerns.

I was busy as a curate in Highgate and had a young family. The children and Mary, my wife, came to the conferences, but I had too little time and Tom Dalton was equally busy. After a short while, in 1967, Olive Dearlove, a very faithful office secretary who travelled from Hove – another Unitarian – resigned. Her place was taken by Kathleen Richards, who had already taken on the organization of the London lecture programme. Miss Richards became honorary general secretary. She had enormous enthusiasm and sent long, friendly handwritten letters to anyone who showed any interest in WCF. She could write equally long, irate letters when she disagreed with the officers or the executive! Several members gave her voluntary help, especially Gladys Ludbrook, who was an active Unitarian and deeply committed member of WCF, and who was at every conference welcoming members, giving them their badges and telling them their room numbers.

Gradually Tom Dalton found himself able to give less and less time to WCF and resigned in 1968. By this time, the Revd Eirion Phillips, Minister of Essex Hall Unitarian Church in Notting Hill, had become treasurer. The Revd John Rowland, in his time as treasurer, had patiently conducted the negotiations that led to the sale of Younghusband House and also the revision of the constitution required by the Charity Commissioners.

In 1972, Lord Sorensen died. After a while, George Appleton, who was at the time Anglican Archbishop in Jerusalem, agreed to become chairman. Dr Edward Carpenter, who was president, deputized until Appleton retired from Jerusalem and returned to Britain in 1974. On his return, George Appleton gave considerable attention to WCF.

Appleton, as we have seen, had been active in WCF in the late fifties and early sixties. Indeed, throughout his life he was concerned for sympathetic understanding between the faiths of the world. An unusual and varied ministry brought him into contact with people of many faiths. He served his curacy in Stepney, where forty per cent of the parishioners were Jewish. Almost in the first week, his rector said to him: 'Tomorrow is the Day of Atonement. You had better attend the closing hour of it in the synagogue in Rectory Square. I will arrange it with my friend, the rabbi. Don't forget to wear a hat.'[1] Two years later, in 1927, Appleton was on his way as a missionary to Burma, where he was to serve until after the Second World War. In the fifties, he became a secretary of the conference of British Missionary Societies. Then, after working in the city of London, he became Archbishop of Perth in Western Australia and then Anglican Archbishop in Jerusalem, a position which involved extensive travelling throughout the Middle East.

George Appleton had high hopes for WCF, although lack of resources largely frustrated them. He believed that WCF had a unique role:

It could become the ecumenical centre of the various religious societies. We could make a contribution to world peace if we could only get representatives of the religions thinking together

L to R: The Revd Marcus Braybrooke, Bishop George Appleton,
Professor Harmindar Singh and Dame Eileen Younghusband

about the problems of peace and war, about the homeless and
the hungry.

He hoped conferences could be held in different countries. He
thought WCF should seek to co-operate with UNA, UNESCO, the
World Council of Churches, the Temple of Understanding and
other bodies. WCF needed to establish an inter-religious
information bureau along the lines of Interreligio in the
Netherlands. Appleton also suggested an award along the lines of
the Nobel Peace Prize for the greatest contribution to interfaith
understanding.[2]

In a sermon that he preached at my church in Frindsbury,
Kent, he outlined why he felt the encounter of religions was so
urgent. There was greater contact between people of different
faiths; the non-Christian faiths had undergone a great revival;
people everywhere were concerned about the condition of the
world with its widespread war, want and hunger; the worldwide
missionary activity of the Church had stimulated thinking on the

most profound questions, whilst the scientific outlook had led to a
questioning of all religion. Archbishop Appleton then sketched
a world history of the development of religions, leading to the
encounter and dialogue of the present century. He suggested that
Christians should look for signs of God's activity in all religions
and believe that Jesus Christ is relevant to all, whilst expecting to
learn more of God from others. The aim he said was

> not to amalgamate all religions in one syncretistic man-made
> religion, but to provoke one another towards the ultimate
> truth, emulate one another in love and service and work
> together for a new order in the affairs of men, when the vision
> of God's good world shall come closer to fulfilment and men
> shall live together in peace, enjoying the wonderful world that
> God and men together can make possible.[3]

In another sermon, preached in Canterbury Cathedral during the
fortieth anniversary conference of WCF, Appleton suggested that
'each religion has a mission, a gospel, a central affirmation . . .
good news not only for its own people but for all humanity'. He
gave, hesitantly, some examples:

> The Muslim emphasis on the sovereignty of God and the duty
> of submission to the will of Allah; the Jewish loyalty to the
> Torah, the Law of the Lord for both individual and national
> life, insights and obligations for man in society; the Hindu
> faith that the spirit of man and the Spirit of the Universe are
> akin, *Tat Tvam Asi*; the Zoroastrian insight that personal life
> and human history are a never-ending struggle between the
> good and the evil, truth and the lie; the Buddha's diagnosis of
> the desire and greed, lust and attachment that is at the root
> of man's frustration and suffering, and that the way of
> freedom lies through following the Noble Eight-fold Path; the
> Christian belief that God manifested himself, his nature and
> his will in Jesus of Nazareth, whose acceptance of the Cross
> revealed the unlimited love of God.

'Each of us', he concluded, 'needs to enlarge on the gospel which he
has received, without wanting to demolish the gospel of others.'[4]

In an attempt to raise the public profile of WCF, George Appleton suggested that HH the Dalai Lama and Yehudi Menuhin (now Lord Menuhin) should be invited to succeed Dr Radhakrishnan as patrons of WCF. Both accepted the invitation. Another suggestion Appleton made was that WCF should arrange a large meeting with major speakers. He agreed to fly back from Jerusalem himself to participate. An approach was made to Michael Ramsey, the Archbishop of Canterbury, as to whether he would agree to speak. His letter declining the invitation reveals the suspicions of WCF that were widespread in the Anglican Church at that time. 'I cannot', Ramsey wrote, 'honestly see myself happily taking part in a function of this kind, especially when the World Congress of Faiths is the sponsoring body.'

Ramsey's first objection was that, although Christians should show reverence towards other faiths, he did not believe that 'religion' was a banner under which all should unite as if it contained the essence of what is good versus 'irreligion' as its opposite. 'Not all "religion" is good, and some of the religion under the Hindu banner seems to be very bad indeed.' He was willing to join in a human rights platform, but not a 'religions' platform. His other objection was that he felt the 'World Congress of Faiths ideology is being used by non-Christian religions in order to propagate their own belief in a "diffused" view of deity and revelation at the expense of the distinctive Christian belief in particularity.'

Dr Edward Carpenter, as president, wrote a detailed and careful reply. He rejected the view, held by some of WCF's critics, that it was trying to create a new eclectic religion: 'Respect for mutual integrity is recognised as the condition of a worthwhile dialogue . . . For myself I am more fully seized of this very particularity since I have come to know more about other faiths.' Dr Carpenter asserted that WCF's aim was to encourage dialogue between 'mainstream' groups.

Carpenter then said the purpose of the proposed meeting was 'that at a time of division and fratricidal strife, the great faiths of the world, within their continuing witness in depth, ought to be able to contribute something to the healing of the world's ills'. He continued that it had never occurred to him that there was any suggestion that humanists and Marxists were not also concerned about human rights. He ended on a more personal note, saying that he had hoped that those who tried to implement WCF's stated policy had the Archbishop's support.

The Archbishop, in his reply on 17 November 1969, admitted that 'I think it was unfair of me to use the phrase "the Congress of Faiths ideology" and I was using words vaguely and inaccurately. I should perhaps have said "some of the things said from within the World Congress of Faiths".' Dr Ramsey then reiterated his main objection about presenting a platform of 'religion' as the way forward for humanity, 'as I am not really sure that it is'.[5]

Despite this disappointment the meeting went ahead at Central Hall, Westminster, on 11 December 1970. A good-sized audience attended. The speakers were eminent, but perhaps not quite famous enough for the meeting to make the impact that had been hoped for. The speakers were Dr Baldoon Dhingra, a Hindu scholar on the staff of UNESCO; Ven. Chao Khun Sobhane Dhammasudhi, head of the Buddhist Vipassana Centre in the UK; Dr Barnett Joseph, director for Jewish–Christian Relations in the Chief Rabbi's office; Sir Muhammad Zafrulla Khan, president of the International Court of Justice at The Hague; Indarjit Singh, at the time editor of the *Sikh Courier* and Archbishop Appleton, Dr Edward Carpenter and Lord Sorensen.

In an effort to make the organization of WCF more effective, Bishop Appleton introduced the Revd Jack Austin, a Buddhist, as development officer. Jack Austin was seconded by the National Westminster Bank for two years. Kathleen Richards soon left. This meant that in effect Jack Austin took on the duties of secretary and had too little time for development work. For a time, he had the help of Rita Wing as office secretary. Once again, lack of finance hampered the hoped-for expansion and no decisive action was taken on a report by Elizabeth Montgomery Campbell, a management consultant. Jack Austin worked hard to build up WCF as a centre of information. This required time to collect and collate information, as well as time to respond to enquiries – work now handled, far more effectively and with greater resources, by the Inter Faith Network for the UK. At the time, the WCF office did not have a computer.

At the end of his second year, Jack Austin wrote an extensive report about his work, detailing the many chores he had to undertake. He emphasized that it was 'the quality and number of staff available which determines what is actually done'. It was only when Rita Wing joined the staff that he had time to do anything about development. He weeded out lapsed members, insisted that the subscription should be raised to £5 and started to enrol new members. Looking ahead, he suggested the need for close co-operation between the various interfaith groups, with the journal *World Faiths* acting as a link. He felt the Congress should concentrate on its annual conference and Younghusband Lecture and try to build up more local groups. Austin drew attention to the lack of money: although WCF balanced its books, the small income made real development impossible. WCF was not, he said, a world body and should call itself 'the Inter-Faith Fellowship', 'which is what it really is'.[6]

When Jack Austin resigned, he was succeeded by Sister Teresa of the Anglican Community of St Andrew. The arrangement was that she should work half time for the Congress, which would pay an honorarium to her community. An American, Sister Teresa was energetic and knowledgeable. Dressed in a habit, she rode a powerful motorbike. Increasingly her many other interests, especially her concern for the position of the diaconate in the church, left her with too little time. It was a serious loss for WCF when she resigned as secretary in 1981.

For part of her time, I worked with her as chairman. When Bishop Appleton resigned in 1978, he suggested that I should succeed him. I was at the time rector of Swainswick and Langridge, near Bath. At thirty-nine, I was the youngest person to become chairman of WCF. I had a detailed knowledge of the working of the Congress, but lacked the public profile of previous chairmen. The feeling was that WCF needed someone who could give quite a lot of time to the Congress rather than a well-known figure, with little time and no previous knowledge of WCF.

The vice-chairman was Rabbi Hugo Gryn, of the West London Synagogue. Hugo Gryn, who was born in Czechoslovakia, spent his teenage years in a concentration camp. He has worked tirelessly through many organizations to combat racism and to promote interfaith understanding. He has been chairman of the Standing Conference on Inter Faith Dialogue in Education and, with Bishop Jim Thompson, was a first co-chair of the Inter Faith Network. I also worked closely with Brian Reep, who was the treasurer. Deeply committed to Sir Francis's vision, Brian Reep gave a lot of time to WCF and served on the executive for many years. He has also worked hard for interfaith co-operation in Surrey, where he lives. He had carefully thought-out plans to put WCF's finances on a sound footing, but sadly his hopes were not fully realized.

During Sister Teresa's time as secretary, the office was moved to a 'ground-floor' or basement office below the hall of All Saints Church, Notting Hill. At first the office was quite convenient. Sister Teresa's community was nearby. The rector of All Saints, the Revd Randolph Wise, who became Dean of Peterborough, was sympathetic to WCF and his wife, Hazel, worked part time as WCF's office secretary. The hall was available for WCF meetings. Many members, however, found the location difficult and in later years there was less rapport with the Church authorities. Various time-consuming efforts to find another office all came to nothing, until the decision was made to move the office to Oxford in 1993.

Sister Teresa's and Hazel Wise's departure created considerable difficulties. Margot Morse was appointed secretary. A very capable person who had held an important administrative job, she found the lack of office facilities frustrating and also suffered from quite a lot of illness. By this time, I had taken up a position as Director of Training in the Diocese of Bath and Wells and was living in Wells. With the acquiescence of John Bickersteth, the Bishop of Bath and Wells, my part-time secretary, Veronica Whitehead, in order to ensure that WCF's essential work continued, typed quite a lot of letters on WCF notepaper!

After a time, Margot Morse felt unable to continue and, in 1983, Patricia Morrison, a New Zealander, who had just retired as international secretary of YWCA (The Young Women's Christian Association) became secretary. She brought to WCF wide international experience and a deep interest in WCF's objectives. She represented WCF at a range of related activities, but it was difficult to combine this outreach with the administrative demands. Despite a variety of voluntary help, there was not the money to provide her with the proper secretarial assistance that she deserved. As a result, she had to do much of the routine office work, which meant that she became very over-burdened. Once again financial constraints frustrated WCF's efforts to expand its work.

In 1983, soon after Patricia Morrison had taken over as secretary, I felt it was time to hand on the chairmanship. I had found the task of ensuring that the office kept going wearying, especially as living in Somerset meant that I was not as readily available to visit the office and to attend meetings in London as I would have wished. There was also a possibility that I might have taken up work in Israel, at the Ecumenical Institute at Tantur. In fact in 1984 I was invited to become director of the Council of Christians and Jews, so it would have been inappropriate to have remained chairman of WCF.

A further difficulty had been suggestions from both the Unification Church to work with them in their interfaith work and from Michael Woodard to co-operate with the World Order for Cultural Exchange that he hoped to create. These discussions took a lot of time, caused division within WCF because of suspicions about the credibility of both the Unification Church and of the World Order for Cultural Exchange, and were fruitless. Whilst the WCF has never agreed to joint sponsorship of events with the Unification Church, individual members have made their own decisions on whether or not to attend interfaith events sponsored by that Church. Although many of Michael Woodard's ideas were imaginative, the World Order for Cultural Exchange proved to be a 'one-man show' and did not survive his death.

Lord Combermere, who was in charge of the religious studies programme of London University extra-mural department, agreed to become chairman. He brought to WCF his wide experience in adult education and ensured that WCF's programme of conferences and lectures was of a high academic standard. The link with the extra-mural department of London University has continued. Lord Combermere's wife, Jill, was very supportive. Her father is R. G. Coulson, in 1996 aged over ninety-five, who, as we have seen, tried in the fifties to introduce interfaith contemplative prayer meetings into the life of WCF.

When Patricia Morrison felt it was time to retire and to return to New Zealand, Tom Gulliver, a member of the Society of Friends who had worked for several years for Toc H and who had

# LAMBETH PALACE

## NOVEMBER 21st 1983

# RECITAL
### By

# ROSALIND
# RUNCIE

IN AID OF
**THE WORLD CONGRESS
OF FAITHS**

In 1983 a concert was held at Lambeth Palace to raise money for WCF
[Courtesy Haro Hodson]

long been active in WCF, agreed to take on the running of WCF,
assisted for a time by Pauline Astor. This involved his travelling up
from near Bournemouth, although he often stayed a night in
London. He gave great attention to the future organization of

WCF. The Trustees Association was wound up, the constitution was revised and preparations made for 'a change of gear'.

Professor Keith Ward, a very distinguished Anglican theologian, then professor at King's College, London and now Regius Professor at the University of Oxford, had become chairman. It was agreed to appoint, in place of Tom Gulliver and at his suggestion, a part-time, paid director, Lesley Matthias, and also in the office a part-time paid secretary, Helen Garton. This was to some extent a gamble as the payments would come out of reserves whilst fresh money was raised. It was felt that it was essential to increase the activities of WCF and to raise its profile if it was to attract money. Lesley Matthias, therefore, was asked to develop a forward-looking programme. However, there were difficulties. One was the growing recession in Britain, which meant that donations to charities were being cut back, so it was a particularly difficult time to raise new money. Secondly, Lesley Matthias was living in Peterborough, where she worked part time at the College of Higher Education. This made it difficult to co-ordinate her work with that of the office. Thirdly, it took time to plan a new approach and programme and not all existing members of WCF were enthusiastic about the changes. Sadly, new money did not become available in the amounts required. It was unrealistic to have hoped that Lesley Matthias might both develop a new programme and have time to do serious fund-raising. An experienced fund-raiser gave good advice, but there was no one to do the work.

Lesley Matthias, whose own previous experience of interfaith activity was mainly in a local interfaith group at Peterborough, was clear that WCF needed a new focus:

The dynamic of inter-religious relations is changing daily. There is need for urgent action to prevent the deterioration of inter-religious relations to a point where 'communalism' becomes an evident dynamic of British society. WCF needs to take up this challenge and engage in those areas of inter-religious relations – even conflict, where the need is most urgent and where the impact of the organisation can be most felt. WCF should be prepared to change its historical emphases in an attempt to meet these new demands. The emphases of the past have been to promote a spirit of fellowship and to engage in the field very approximately described as 'comparative religion'. There has been an emphasis on that which religions tend to hold in common and perhaps an emphasis on the spiritual and personal dimensions of religious experience. For WCF to meet the needs of the religiously plural society of the nineties, there have to be new emphases and directions.

The interfaith movement, she continued, 'has generally acquired the image of a "hobby horse" of the "liberals" and "enlightened" members of major religious traditions and those of none. It has become wrongly seen by many as an activity undertaken by those at the fringes of their own religious traditions rather than as a commitment undertaken as part of a mainstream tradition.' This, she added, 'is largely a wrong perception'. At the same time, she suggested, there had been a deterioration in inter-religious relations in Britain, and especially the scapegoating of Muslims.

WCF should, Matthias argued, focus on the 'immediate issues which arise out of the practical outworkings of a maturing plural society'. Some of these issues she identified as the relationship between religion and politics, the pastoral and spiritual care of religious minority groups, for example in prisons, the responsibility of the media, difficulties of the individual believer in relation to mixed marriage and the feasibility of common worship.

As director, Lesley Matthias tried to move the WCF programme to address some of these matters. This has continued. A WCF working group is preparing a resource book on multifaith worship, a conference has been held on mixed-faith families and the religious identity of their children. The 1994 Younghusband Lecture grappled with some of the passionate reactions to the suffering in former Yugoslavia. The practical relevance of an understanding of the world's religions to many aspects of current British life is being increasingly recognized and it is right for WCF to address this concern. A question not dealt with in Lesley Matthias's paper 'A Strategy for the Future' is how WCF's work relates to that of other bodies concerned for good interfaith relations, which are tackling similar issues.[7]

Financial problems denied Lesley Matthias the opportunity

to implement her proposals. By 1992, it was clear that WCF was not in a position to guarantee the salary of a part-time director and a part-time secretary. Keith Ward by this time had moved to Oxford and wished to give up as chairman, because of the even greater demands upon his time in his new position. He accepted an invitation to become joint president with Dr Edward Carpenter. In 1992, I agreed to become chairman for a second time. I had recently resigned as non-stipendiary vicar of Christ Church, Bath, so had a little more time. I was also much involved in the international plans for the 1993 Year of Inter-religious Understanding and Co-operation and wished to see an accompanying programme in Britain. David Potter, who had been honorary treasurer since 1987, agreed to combine with this the task of administrator, and his wife, Jean, has taken on increasing responsibility for the programme, as well as for *One Family*. Both have given a great deal of time and devoted service to WCF. Mae Marven, Brenda Fischel and Annette Marco and others gave an enormous amount of voluntary help in the office.

At the end of 1993, as part of the plan to establish an international interfaith centre in Oxford, the office was moved to Market Street, Oxford, in a building shared with the International Association for Religious Freedom and the International Interfaith Centre. Diana Hanmer, who had been a part-time secretary to Bishop Appleton, became part-time office secretary. Financial and administrative control remained with David Potter. Together with Jean Potter, I have taken on some of the responsibilities of the director. In 1996, after seven years' conscientious work, David Potter was succeeded by David Storey as honorary treasurer and by Shahin Bekhradnia as honorary secretary.

With these changes has gone a change in WCF's self-understanding. The inability to sustain the expansion programme of the late eighties has meant that WCF now is largely dependent on voluntary labour. David Potter has overseen a slimming down of administration. WCF is also clearly a fellowship of individual members. This distinguishes it from The Inter Faith Network for the UK which is for organizations. Some of the work that WCF attempted to do in the seventies and early eighties is now much better done by the Network.

Is WCF still necessary? In my view, yes. Because it is a

fellowship of individuals committed to interfaith friendship, it has a freedom that a more official body such as the Network does not have. This means that WCF can and should take a pioneering role, and it is able to articulate a point of view that might not be shared by the designated leadership of faith communities. For example, the WCF publication on multifaith worship will deal with a controversial subject and one with which some faith communities are uneasy. The conference on the spiritual and pastoral care of the dying in a multifaith society opened up a new area. WCF also offers those individuals who are engaged in interfaith work a chance to meet co-workers, to reflect together on their concerns and to be renewed in their endeavours. Probably in any local group there are three or four people who are really keen and maintain the local group's activities. WCF can offer them the stimulus and encouragement they need. This depends on WCF offering a programme of a high quality.

As interfaith activities increase, it becomes clearer that there are different motivations and agendas. Whilst WCF has always affirmed the integrity and distinctiveness of the world religions and has repudiated syncretism, it has also been conscious of the mystical tradition, voiced by Younghusband, which suggests a meeting in the spirit. The arrangement of retreat weekends where people of different faiths can explore each other's spiritual disciplines is an expression of this dimension. This again gives a special emphasis to WCF's activities.

## Mid-life crisis

'The World Congress of Faiths is suffering from an identity crisis,' wrote Nikki Malet de Carteret in one of the many reports on future strategies for WCF. 'Many' may be an exaggeration. There were, in fact, three reports by consultants, but many more comments and papers by officers and staff. The first report was by Elizabeth Montgomery Campbell in 1973, the second by Nikki de Carteret in 1987 and the third by Pauline Astor in 1989. They all sprang from a desire that WCF should become a larger, professionally run organization, which meant that it would need to raise considerable amounts of money. It was assumed that no 'holy men' of any faith would know about money and that it was essential to have the advice of business consultants. The real problem has been that faith communities have not so far been willing to make significant resources available for interfaith work.

The previous section has told of the changes of personnel and the failure 'to change gear'. The reports are worth further consideration because they raise questions about different expectations of 'interfaith dialogue' and should be of interest to many people beyond WCF members.

I have to admit to being a little sceptical about consultants' reports! The purpose of the WCF has always seemed clear to me, as has the fact that it is likely to remain a fairly small group of individuals who sense a spiritual unity that transcends religious differences. Re-reading the reports, however, I recognize that others had different expectations. As a parish priest, I have also spent much of my life working with volunteers, so am less confident that 'professionalization' (to use a consultant's term!) is a solution to all problems.

Nonetheless, all the reports are carefully prepared and astute in their comments. They reflect the varied motivation of different members of the Congress, which in turn illuminate the different understandings of and approaches to interfaith work.

Elizabeth Montgomery Campbell makes much of the different objectives of the original (1936) constitution and those adopted in 1966.

The 1936 objectives were:

1. To promote a spirit of fellowship among mankind through religion.
2. To awaken and develop world loyalty while allowing complete freedom for diversities of men, nations and faiths.

The 1966 objective was:

To advance religious education by promoting knowledge and understanding of the beliefs and practices of the religious faiths, sects and denominations of the world by promoting the study of comparative religion.

As I recall, the 1966 objectives were adopted reluctantly because the Charity Commissioners indicated that promoting a spirit of fellowship was not in itself charitable. It was felt at the time that religious education – a term acceptable to the Charity Commissioners – would promote a spirit of fellowship. John Rowland's comments at the extraordinary meeting, at which the constitutional amendments were approved, and a subsequent note by Heather McConnell confirm my memory. Members who voted for the changes did not see them as marking any significant alteration in the purposes of WCF, but as necessary to retain the tax advantages of being a charity. This is why some of those interviewed by Elizabeth Montgomery Campbell 'were obviously not aware of the limitations suggested by the amended objects'.

Elizabeth Montgomery Campbell rightly recognized that some members retained an international outlook, whilst others were content to focus on the British situation. This meant that, in her view, the name *World* Congress of Faiths was misleading. In fact, as she noted, by the seventies, when her report was written, Britain's concern for the Empire was decreasing, whilst Britain was itself becoming a multifaith society. What, she asked, was WCF's role?

Is WCF's primary role to work for world peace and world loyalty, as the founder envisaged when Britain was a world power with a vast Empire?

Is it to promote the academic study of comparative religion for its own sake, within the narrow limits of the 1966 objects?

Is it to promote mutual understanding and tolerance between British citizens of different ethnic origins, by helping them to understand and respect one another's faiths and cultures?

Is it all three, and if so, in what order?

Elizabeth Montgomery Campbell clearly thought the third option was the most relevant, especially as the SHAP Working Party on World Religions in Education was taking on the second task.[8]

Nikki de Carteret also felt that the 1936 objectives were

inspired by 'the romanticism and idealism' of the Empire, yet it is interesting how such a concern has today again become widespread as we adjust to living in a global society. Hans Küng's phrase 'no world peace without peace between the religions' is widely quoted. Nikki de Carteret recognized the different concerns of members: 'Is WCF's role to bring people of different religions together? Is it to inspire spiritual experience? Is it to educate? Or to foster academic study? Or is it all of these? Can the organization be all things to all men and women?' The lack of clarity about WCF's purpose, she argued, made it hard to project WCF to a wider audience.

Nikki de Carteret recognized that if WCF remained as it was, it would only attract the liberals within religions and 'seekers'. She recognized the importance of interfaith dialogue to communities divided by fear and suspicion, and acknowledged the important role in this of the then newly established Inter Faith Network of the UK. If WCF wished to grow significantly it would, in her view, need to become more popular and focus more on religious community relations.[9]

The Carteret report again made clear the need for a full-time paid director and the raising of the necessary funds for this. A chairman's appeal for £50,000, however, met with an 'extremely disappointing' response and the appointment of a director was put 'on hold'.

The report by Pauline Astor was an attempt to move things forward. She noted three weaknesses: a 'muddled identity, a lack of enthusiastic committed support and a lack of funds'. She suggested three ways forward: either to remain as it was and to continue to decline, to seek a merger with a larger body or to create a team of workers and to appoint a paid director.[10]

Efforts were made to set up a number of sub-groups, so as to involve more people in the work of WCF and to increase activity. Tom Gulliver, as honorary secretary, worked tirelessly to build the basis on which WCF could move forward or 'change gear'. In 1990, it was decided to go ahead and advertise for a part-time director and a part-time secretary. Some money had been raised but no source had been found to guarantee their salaries for at least three years. It was hoped that a new image and greater activity would generate fresh income. In fact, despite several meetings, no real fund-raising campaign was undertaken and the recession meant that new money was extremely difficult to find. The position was not helped by the cancellation of the 1991 annual conference. Lesley Matthias took up her post as part-time executive director in the autumn of 1990, but by the autumn of 1992, WCF, having eaten into its reserves, was no longer able to guarantee a salary. She returned to her college teaching. The hope was that she would continue as programme director on an honorary basis, but it soon became obvious that she did not have the time to do this.

WCF is now clear that it is an organization for individual members. The journal and newsletter are important endeavours. Conferences are organized, often with the extra-mural department of London University. The aim is to explore in depth matters that other organizations might find it difficult to treat. Its influence will be in terms of the quality of its thinking; it will be listened to if it has anything significant to say.

My own view is that Younghusband's intention was that WCF should help people of different faiths to discover a mystical unity which transcends particular religious traditions. Such an awareness of human unity would inspire a concern for peace. Had the aim just been the study of religions there was no reason to establish WCF, given that the Society for the Study of the Great Religions, in which Younghusband was active, already was in existence.

Younghusband's intention was quickly perceived by critics as 'syncretistic', although this was consistently denied by members of WCF. If syncretism means an attempt to create one world religion, this has never been WCF's aim. If the aim is that members of each religion should recognize a spiritual affinity with members of other religions this *was* Younghusband's intention. His efforts rested upon a mystical understanding of religious experience and religious truth.

Not all who are concerned for good interfaith relations share this approach. There is an important difference between those for whom the starting point is the conviction that there is a transcendent unity and those who stress the real differences, which require people to find a way of living together harmoniously. The latter view seems to have been emphasized by WCF in the late eighties and early nineties – partly to get away from WCF's 'syncretistic' image and partly to focus on the community relations dimension of living in a multifaith society. With this went a concern not to offend members of so-called 'mainstream' religious groups by encouraging seekers or members of 'new religions' to take an active part in WCF. My own view is that genuine spiritual experience may well be found in newer groups as well as in more traditional communities. Several new groups, such as Brahma Kumaris, have a strong sense of the fellowship of faiths.

The hesitation to relate to new groups is shown in the correspondence and minutes of the late eighties. It reflects the deep suspicion that some WCF members harboured towards 'New Age' spirituality. There was equal suspicion of new religions. This was shown in the sharp criticism of the London group when it arranged a series of talks by members of new groups such as Unificationists and Scientologists. Earlier, the WCF executive had agreed that members of any group could join WCF, although the executive retained the right to suspend the membership of anyone found to be using WCF meetings for proselytism or political activity – a power which has so far never been exercised.

These are issues that remain unresolved. Whilst WCF has not set boundaries on who should join, and 'seekers' have always been welcome, its primary task is to build up fellowship between members of the world religions. This means that it is important to try to ensure a proper balance to the membership, which of course is difficult in an organization based on individual membership.

The proper balance between recognizing a spiritual affinity between religions and avoiding syncretism is also difficult, as the enormous amount of literature on this subject indicates. WCF has always been careful to avoid defining the relationship between religions. Its emphasis has been on building good relations between *people* who belong to different religions.

It is this that perhaps makes its purpose distinct from semi-official bodies, such as the Inter Faith Network for the UK, the departments for 'other religions' of religious or denominational bodies, and from university departments for the academic study of religions. WCF has been, and still is, a fellowship of spiritual pioneers. Together, as we shall see, they have explored many different aspects of the coming together of people of faith.

# 8. 'Lectures, Chat and Lukewarm Coffee': conferences and lectures

There are various stages to building friendship between people of different faiths. Often people have false or prejudicial views about members of other religions. In part, this can be countered by the production of accurate books about the world religions or by lectures which give correct information. It is even more important to meet members of other faiths and to visit their places of worship. As trust and friendship grows, people begin to discuss common problems and to share their experiences of faith. They may discover concerns that they have in common and take action together. They may wish to meditate and pray together.

Because the growth of interfaith friendship has different stages and each person has to travel this journey for herself or himself, the programme of the World Congress of Faiths has tried to cater for a variety of needs. Its work has been primarily educational, arranging conferences, lectures and tours and publishing a journal and other literature.

## Conferences

Lady Ravensdale once said: 'I sometimes think that our congress has been a series of good lectures, chat and lukewarm cups of coffee.'[1] Conferences have been of three main types: large conferences with a high level of intellectual content; quiet, smaller conferences of a retreat character for spiritual sharing; and conferences to meet with members of local multifaith communities.

It would be tedious to try to summarize all the conferences; all that can be done is to mention a few. We have already glanced at the pre-war conferences. Even during the Second World War and immediately afterwards, efforts were made to arrange an annual conference, which has continued to be important in the life of the Congress, although its nature has changed over the years.

The 1951 Oxford conference seems to have been remarkable for the quality of the papers. Professor André Toledano from

France mentioned his initial surprise that, 'at a time when mankind is living in the dreadful fear of a grim future', the conference did not address economic or political questions. 'But on second thoughts', he continued, 'I realised that a religious meeting should deal with what is of permanent value for mankind; beauty, health, the body and the spirit and, to finish with, the defence of the spirit fighting with matter in industry.' Even so, he remained surprised that one session was devoted to 'The Religious Attitude to Animal Welfare'. The session changed his mind. 'In our time of hatred and contempt for the human person, recalling the reverence due to all the creatures that God made was most inspiring.'[2] Canon L. W. Grensted, Regius Professor at Oxford, gave a paper on 'Religion and Healing'. Professor Alistair Hardy, Professor of Marine Biology, who was to do pioneering work on religious experience, led a discussion.

One person at the conference was critical that, at the service, only Christian prayers were used. In fact, as was pointed out to her, prayers were drawn from Christian, Jewish, Muslim and Zoroastrian sources. As the *Forum* editorial comments: 'Prayer unites the ages, it unites the faiths, it unites all mankind.'[3]

In 1955, a European conference, organized together with the World Alliance for Friendship through Religion, was held at Diekirch in Luxembourg. There was obviously dissatisfaction with the hotel accommodation, in particular that there was no hot water. The addresses on the subject of 'Spiritual Experience and Moral Responsibilities' were of a high standard. Joan Dopping felt it was one of the most vigorous WCF events for some years.

## A conference at Bremen

Two years later, a conference was held with the German branch at Bremen. Some two hundred people attended. From Britain there was a small group which included Lady Ravensdale, Arthur Peacock and George Appleton. The opening address on 'The Unity and Collaboration of Religions' was by Professor Friedrich Heiler of Marburg. Deploring the exclusiveness in some religions, including Christianity, he mentioned a number of Christians in different generations who had had a broader outlook. He then listed seven points held in common by the higher faiths. These were:

1. the reality of the transcendent;
2. the immanence of the transcendent in our human heart;
3. this reality as the highest truth – *summum bonum*;
4. the revelation of the divine love and mercy in man;
5. the way to the divine reality by sacrifice, prayer and meditation;
6. the unity of love towards God and one's neighbour;
7. the last aim: perfection of the soul in God's infinity.

One of Heiler's pupils, Annemarie Schimmel, spoke about 'The Importance of Islamic Mysticism for the Unity of Religions', whilst Pastor Engelhardt spoke about Rabindranath Tagore. The Revd George Appleton warned that there was perhaps a tendency at the conference to assume that more had been achieved than was in fact the case: 'We were only at a beginning and the encounter and confrontation of different religions in a spirit of mutual tolerance must go on,' he said. This encounter, he believed, was in the purposes of God.

A particularly moving moment was when Heiler paid tribute to the Grand Rabbi of Luxembourg for his willingness to return to Germany from which he had had to flee many years before. The Grand Rabbi spoke on 'Judaism and the Unity of Religions' and explained that the idea of 'a chosen people', which was often misunderstood, was not inimical to the aims of the conference.[4]

*Bristol, 1969*

The centre pages of *World Faiths*, No. 77, contain pictures of the WCF conference held in 1969 at Wills Hall, Bristol. The subject was 'Moral Standards Today'. Speakers included Ven. Boonchuay, a Buddhist monk, and Albert Polack, who for several years was education officer of the Council of Christians and Jews. The conference concluded with a memorable service at which the preacher was Lord Sorensen – some of whose sermon has already

Kathleen Richards and George Harrison with other WCF members at a conference [Stearn & Sons]

been quoted.[5] The conference included a visit to the tomb of Rajah Ram Mohun Roy, the great Indian reformer and founder of the Brahmo Samaj, and also to the seventeenth-century Lewins Mead Unitarian Chapel, at which Keshub Chander Sen, another leading Hindu reformer, had preached in the last century.

Looking back through past copies of the journal, one comes across a galaxy of well-known speakers who have participated in WCF conferences. They have included Professor Ursula King, now of Bristol University, on 'Mysticism and Feminism', Dr Frank Lake, founder of Clinical Theology, at a conference on 'Wholeness and Healing', Professor Zaehner, former Spalding Professor at Oxford, on the 'Dangers of Mysticism', and Dr Martin Israel, a well-known author and mystic, on 'The Scientific View and the Mystical Vision'.

The subjects discussed are very varied. It is impossible to try to summarize all these conferences, although each one brings back vivid memories for me of people whom I have been privileged to meet. The most I can attempt is to give a glimpse of these gatherings and to look again at questions raised about the nature of dialogue, which are of continuing interest.

## The fortieth anniversary conference

At the fortieth anniversary conference held at Canterbury in 1976, speakers included Ven. Thich Nhat Hahn, Professor Harbans Singh, Bishop George Appleton, Dr Ezra Spicehandler and the Lord Abbot Kosho Ohtani.

Two personal comments on the Canterbury conference are still significant. Pamela McCormack (Pamela Wylam), who had first attended a WCF conference in 1962, had the feeling 'that we have been here before, meeting old friends and repeating the same discussion', although she added that the circle had grown. Marian de Fossard (now Marian Tewkesbury) was at a WCF conference for the first time. She wondered whether the

> talk about what should be done might be greater than works accomplished . . . I realised two needs arising from serious membership of such a group. The first is an individual one of inner growth through knowledge and experience of other faiths . . . The other need is a collective one which necessitates activity of the group, recognition and influence, in a world that is being approached and moulded by a thousand other voices crying 'change'.

The problem then, as Marian de Fossard said, is how religions relate to politics.

The further question is to what extent a religion is an entity. As Ven. Thich Nhat Hahn, a Vietnamese Buddhist teacher, said:

> We are here to meet each other. I cannot imagine how religions can meet each other but I can imagine how people of various faiths meet each other . . . If religion is only knowledge of religion, meeting is not necessary. What we need is only an exchange of books; but we are not books, we are human beings, and that is why the meetings of human beings are very different from meetings of books.

He also questioned whether we necessarily get on better with people within our own religion or 'theological circle' than we do with those outside it: 'Because I have several friends who belong to different religious traditions and I know them and I love them and I work with them, I know that this "theological circle" is a very arbitrary thing.'[6]

At the 1989 conference, Dr Paul Williams, a Buddhist who is a lecturer at the University of Bristol, raised a similar question about who are the participants in dialogue. A religious tradition is moulded by its great teachers, but how can there be dialogue with the dead?

> How can there be dialogue with Nagarjuna, with Asanga, or indeed with the Buddha himself? . . . Dialogue is something which occurs between living representatives of religions, not dead ones. For the purposes of religious dialogue the dead live on not in their texts but in their spiritual descendants who appropriate and use the texts.[7]

Dialogue is a meeting of people and the experience of such encounters is for many people the most vivid and lasting memory of a conference.

### A conference on suffering

This is why one of the most profound conferences was on 'Creative Responses to Suffering'(1979), at which the speakers were Professor Donald Nicholl, Ven. Sumedho, Rabbi Hugo Gryn, Dr Frank Chandra and Fr Benedict Ramsden. Each spoke out of his personal experience and warned about the superficiality of much religious talk on the subject. 'Suffering', said Donald Nicholl, 'is unique to each of us and has as many faces as there are human beings.' Fr Benedict Ramsden, an Orthodox priest, began by speaking of experiences of suffering in his own life. He continued:

> Freedom involves pain but the central doctrine of Christianity is that the cost of that pain has been borne by a man who was God. God entered the world to encounter our life and to share it. God entered into the shriek of a man demented by the world's ultimate rejection, and by death's extremities, who

cried out in atheistic despair, 'My God, my God, why have you forsaken me?'

Rabbi Hugo Gryn, after giving a clear summary of Jewish teaching, ended on a personal note: 'Suffering more often than not shatters and weakens and we do not need to be broken or tortured to discover the goodness and the love of God. The creative response to suffering must be compassion.'[8]

## The fiftieth anniversary conference

If dialogue is mostly conducted by words, then the way we use words in our religious life is important. At the 1978 York conference, Professor Maurice Wiles, Regius Professor of Divinity at the University of Oxford, and Dr al-Faruqi, Professor of Islamics at Temple University, Philadelphia, spoke on 'The Language of Faith'. In November 1986, a rather similar subject was discussed at the fiftieth anniversary conference, which was held at the Royal Veterinary College in London. The main speaker was Professor Wilfred Cantwell Smith, Professor Emeritus of the Comparative History of Religion at Harvard University. He argued that:

> First, we cannot speak about even the everyday immediate world without metaphors; let alone, about the transcendent, the ultimate, about God. Secondly, metaphors, as linguistic symbols are marvellous: not to be apologised for, but to be rejoiced in. They are the medium of transcendence *par excellence*; to speak theistically, God Himself speaks to us in metaphors, and more generally, has come to us in and through symbols. Thirdly, if we recognise these facts, we can talk to each other, with grace and effectiveness.

In a challenging closing section of his talk, Wilfred Cantwell Smith asked whom we meant when in a religious community we use the term 'we'. 'The time has come', he said, 'when it is a criterion of moral and spiritual maturity to mean, when saying "we" religiously, "we human beings".' He expressed his unease with the word 'dialogue'. Certainly the idea that 'we Christians are

Mavis and Zaki Badawi

speaking to you Sikhs is an advance on the we/they way of speaking'. Yet religious diversity is a human matter that we confront together. 'Colloquy', he suggested, is a better word: 'We share a common planet and we are jointly in process of constructing a common future . . . The only common goal worth pursuing is one that appeals to us all; and one to the building of which the faith of each one of us can inspire our striving.' Responses on 'The Language of Dialogue' were made by Professor G. S. Mansukhani, Ven. Dr M. Vajiragnana, Professor Seshagiri Rao, Professor Keith Ward, Rabbi Dr Norman Solomon and Dr Zaki Badawi.[9]

*London, 1989*

In 1989 the main speaker was Professor Hans Küng. His subject, which has since become well known through his book *Global Responsibility*, was 'No World Peace without Peace between Religions'. The conference itself, however, was based on his book *Christianity and World Religions*. Responses were made by two Buddhists, Dr Paul Williams and Ven. Dr M. Vajiragnana, by two Muslims, Dr Muhammad Mashuq Ibn Ally and Dr Yaqub Zaki, and by the Hindu scholar Professor Seshagiri Rao.[10]

L to R: Professor Hans Küng with Dr Mashuq Ally and Professor Keith Ward [Carlos Peyes]

The discussion again raised questions about the usefulness of dialogue, especially as one speaker at the conference said: 'Interfaith dialogue is an exercise in futility.' One question was whether the Christian scholars on whom Küng had relied for information about other faiths were accurate. Can a member of one faith really understand another tradition? A second question was, who speaks for a religion? Thirdly, is each religion making a permanent take-over bid for all the rest? Fourthly, if that take-over is not your aim, will you be suspect to other members of your faith community? Does that therefore mean that it is only those willing to be self-critical about their own tradition who are willing to engage in dialogue? This is why helping members of a faith to redefine their attitude to other faiths is important and has been, as we shall see, the subject of several Younghusband Lectures.

## Changing patterns

In recent years, the pattern of conferences has changed for various reasons. In the seventies, well-attended residential conferences were held in different parts of the country. In the eighties, several large non-residential conferences were held in London with well-known speakers. The size, however, and the fact that they were non-residential, meant that whilst the conferences were intellectually stimulating, they lacked the sense of fellowship of earlier gatherings. Large residential conferences present a number of problems. The first is the cost both of residence and of travel. Secondly, younger people especially find it difficult to get away, so that conferences may be arranged mainly for the benefit of the retired. Thirdly, in the last decade, a great number of interfaith meetings have taken place. Often speakers of another faith are invited to events that in a previous generation would have been only for members of the faith that was arranging the event.

This has meant that recent WCF conferences have perhaps been more specialized, because there are now many opportunities for people to gain information about other faiths and to meet with members of those faiths. Local groups, however, are often maintained by the enthusiasm of two or three members. WCF conferences now are perhaps aimed more at providing nourishment for these enthusiasts, allowing those who have considerable experience in this field to pursue issues at a greater depth than may be possible in a local meeting. For example, WCF with the Religious Resource Centre at Derby University has arranged two conferences on 'The Care of the Dying in a Multifaith Society'. At Ammerdown, conferences have been held on multifaith worship and about the needs of members of mixed-faith marriages. WCF arranged, at Peterborough, a conference about the pastoral and spiritual needs of prisoners.

The Derby conferences brought together people from a variety of backgrounds. Some were clergy, imams or rabbis, others were doctors or nurses. There were social workers and volunteer helpers at hospices. The mixture of disciplines as well as of religions was stimulating. The conference soon moved beyond the important questions of ensuring respect for the religious practices of patients to look at the way that the spiritual strength of a believer of one faith could help a believer of another – be he or she a doctor or patient. The conference also heard about the training given to future clergy, rabbis and imams on ministry to the seriously ill.

## Retreats

Some of the small conferences have been retreats designed to encourage personal spiritual growth and appreciation of the inner meaning of religions. In 1972, a small number of people met in the spring in the beautiful city of Durham to share together on the subject of meditation. In the early eighties, a similar emphasis characterized the St Albans Congresses, led by the Revd Peter Dewey and arranged by the Interfaith Association.

Several retreat weekends have been held at the ecumenical centre at Ammerdown, near Bath, which is run by the Sisters of Sion. Bernice Joachim wrote of the first such gathering, which was held in 1976: 'We practised meditation together, several times a day, in quiet waiting, focusing our restless minds on the kingdom within, gently bringing back our life and all its concerns to the Source.'[11] For several years, Bishop George Appleton and Swami Bhavyananda of the Ramakrishna Vedanta Centre were regular leaders of these weekends. Recently, Sandy Martin has arranged retreats at Wantage and at the Ramakrishna Vedanta Centre at Bourne End.

Shahin Bekhradnia, a Zoroastrian and a member of the WCF executive, described her feelings about the Wantage retreat:

The challenging prospect of a silent weekend in retreat attracted me in the first instance. The opportunity to spend it inside a convent further aroused my curiosity, while the chance to be guided through the techniques of different meditation disciplines seemed too good to miss. Above all, the idea of getting away from it all and of just 'being' was precious, although for some, including me, the idea of not talking for the whole weekend, spending two whole days in the company of complete strangers was fairly daunting.[12]

## Experiencing multifaith Britain

WCF has also arranged a number of weekends to give an opportunity for people to experience the multifaith life of some cities, such as Birmingham (1983) or Wolverhampton (1989). Emphasis has been placed on visits to places of worship and on meeting members of different faith communities. Particularly valuable have been the invitations to stay in local homes, with the chance for friendship that this creates.

Those who attended the conference in 1983 at the Multifaith Centre in Birmingham, which was set up by Sister Mary Hall, were given as a souvenir a card which described a person of dialogue:

A person of dialogue experiences the other side, listens to others, learns from them;

A person of dialogue enters completely into the real life situations of people, suffers their lived reality with them;

A person of dialogue gives up power, does not yield to the temptation of imposing ideas, discovers *with* people – not *for* them – what their needs and programmes are;

A person of dialogue meets people on their own terms, in their own time, realising that waiting may well be a more powerful force than acting;

A person of dialogue accepts the fact of not *possessing* the truth or the only right way of doing things, is disposed to the message of others and continuously open to further conversation as a result of dialogue with them;

A person of dialogue develops deep personal relationships, realising that in listening to others, asking them seriously, identifying with their world, he or she is saying Yes to them, affirming them in a way that is tremendously creative, mysteriously salvific;

A person of dialogue is so immersed in the world of others that he or she can begin to ask questions which endorse and which challenge basic human values and, in that context – from within – can announce the good news and denounce sinful structures.[13]

## A *journey in faith*

In 1990, an imaginative interfaith pilgrimage to Iona was arranged. This involved links with many local interfaith groups and stressed both fellowship and the shared spiritual search.

The journey began at the Coronarium at St Katherine's Dock, near Tower Hill, London, where the pilgrims were seen off by the

actress Hayley Mills and by Keith Ward, chair of WCF. The first
night was spent in Derby. The next day, a second send-off was
arranged at Derby Cathedral. The pilgrimage was full of surprises.
In Huddersfield the pilgrims were invited to share in the
celebration of a wedding at Shir Guru Sikh Temple. In Bradford,
they were invited to a mosque for evening prayer.

> Afterwards, we were led to a basement room where large
> white cloths had been spread on the floor. Our hosts
> had prepared a vegetarian meal for us. They had never before
> prepared such a meal and asked, somewhat anxiously, if it
> was all right. It was, in fact, excellent but it was the
> thoughtfulness that lay behind it that moved us. Our hosts
> said that they felt that mutual trust had been established and
> added that they respected Christianity and wished that Islam
> was equally respected by people in this country.

Crossing into Scotland, the pilgrims headed for Iona. The group,
on its way, stayed at the Kagyu Samye Ling Tibetan Buddhist
Centre at Eskdalemuir, in Glasgow and at the Scottish
Churches House at Dunblane.

One pilgrim wrote a prayer, summing up what she had
learned:

> O Great Being, in your wisdom you show yourself within our
> hearts in so many guises. Give us the intelligence not to
> constantly chatter and question everything, but to listen to your
> living answer that we know is the Truth, beating inside us,
> whoever we are, whatsoever we be. Let us see this Truth in
> others, remembering that we share the same plan, the same
> earth, the same cycle, that you have given us. Let us give you
> thanks and praise for giving us love and fellowship as gifts
> to guide us, and hope and trust to inspire us. Help us to
> understand each other, and bring peace to our time.
> Honouring you as you wondrously honour us.[14]

Tom Gulliver, whose idea it was to arrange the pilgrimage, wrote
that perhaps 'the most important lesson of the pilgrimage is that we
found in so many people a longing to meet each other, a hunger no

longer to feel divided by race or culture or religion'.

The value of pilgrimage in interfaith work has been clearly shown by the annual London Multifaith Pilgrimage for Peace, which is arranged by Westminster Interfaith. Sarah Thorley ends her report of the tenth pilgrimage with these words:

> There were also the conversations, wonderful conversations, I shall long remember. I talked with a Hindu about how he grew up in Muslim Rawalpindi and how it feels to be a member of a minority religion. I met a Zoroastrian whose family was originally from Iran; we discussed religious attitudes to the environment. I talked with a Buddhist monk from El Salvador; I spoke with a Malaysian sitar player and a Scottish Jesuit. I talked with a Quaker and his Jewish wife about euthanasia. And I had a long discussion with a Sikh about whether salvation comes through faith or good works!
>
> It was a real celebration of our differences and of how much we share. Different does not have to mean bad or suspect; it can be enriching.[15]

## Younghusband Lectures

In the 1970s, at the suggestion of Bishop Appleton, an annual Sir Francis Younghusband Memorial Lecture was inaugurated. The first lecture was given by K. D. D. Henderson who spoke about Sir Francis Younghusband.

In the eighties, there was a series of Younghusband Lectures in which scholars of different faiths were asked to outline the attitude of their religion to other religions. Each lecturer affirmed the distinct identity of religions and his or her own particular commitment, but in a way that was not exclusive.

Professor Seshagiri Rao used his Younghusband Lecture in 1982 to expound the views of Mahatma Gandhi on the relation of religions. 'Gandhi's inter-religious dialogue authentically represents the Indian attitude of respect for all religions,' he said. 'The idea that "Truth is one: sages call it by different names" has been alive since the time of the *Rgveda* [the earliest Hindu scriptures] . . . To ignore any of the religions meant to ignore God's infinite richness and to impoverish human spirituality.'[16] Similarly, in his 1988

A monk from the London Peace Pagoda with Penny Reynolds and Mae Marven at a Younghusband Lecture  [Peter Reynolds]

Younghusband Lecture, Dr Karan Singh, a devoted worker for inter-religious understanding, after reviewing Hinduism's relationship to several particular religions, ended with a passage that beautifully expressed the Hindu vision of an underlying unity:

At the heart of all the great religious traditions of the world lies a luminous core based upon a certain perception of the divine. By definition, the divine power cannot be confined within any limitations of time or language, scripture or iconography. The great rishis and prophets have all received glimpses of the divinity that pervades the universe, and have sought to express that realization in glowing language. And yet surely it is clear that what they have seen are not different divinities but different aspects of the same all-pervasive divine power, and that the mystic tradition that runs like a golden thread through the world's religions is a powerful unifying force. Just as the sun, reflected in a dozen vessels of differing shapes and sizes, does not lose its unity, so do all the great religions of mankind reflect different aspects of the same divinity.[17]

Dr Zaki Badawi, in his 1984 Younghusband Lecture, started with the assumption that each religion sees its beliefs as final: 'No religious community can allow itself to float in the empty space of uncertainty.' He outlined Islam's view of other religions and suggested that the initial classification of Hinduism as paganism was regrettable. He ended with these words:

> The Muslim accepts differences of belief as a fulfilment of the will of Allah. 'If He so willed He would have made you into one religious community.' He sees in them a manifestation in mankind of the deep feelings of the Eternal. To quote a Sufi poet whom I often quote – who once said addressing the Creator, 'On my way to the Mosque, Oh Lord, I passed the Magian in front of his flame, deep in thought, and a little further I heard a rabbi reciting his holy book in the synagogue, and then I came upon the church where the hymns sung gently in my ears and finally I came into the mosque and watched the worshippers immersed in their experience and I pondered how many are the different ways to You – the one God.[18]

Rabbi Dr Norman Solomon, in his 1985 Younghusband Lecture, suggested that the dialogue of faiths was a natural outgrowth of the mission of Judaism:

> The 'covenant of Noah' offers a pattern for us to seek from others not necessarily conversion to Judaism, but rather faithfulness to the highest principles of justice and morality which we perceive as the essence of revealed religion. I cannot set the bounds of truth, I want to listen and to learn, to grow in experience and forge language, to be open to the world around me and its many people and ways, and to reread and reinterpret my scriptures and the words of the sages constantly, critically, in response to what I learn each day. Only by exposing oneself to such a process can one hope to meet Truth revealed, no granite statue but a living, dynamic force.[19]

L to R: Dr Edward Carpenter, Viscount Combermere, Lord Runcie, Rabbi Hugo Gryn and Sheikh Gamal Soleiman  [Peter Reynolds]

Dr Robert Runcie, the Archbishop of Canterbury, in the 1986 Younghusband Lecture, given to mark the fiftieth anniversary of the Congress, to which reference has already been made, expressed very well the hopes of WCF. Dialogue, he said, 'can help us to recognize that other faiths than our own are genuine mansions of the Spirit with many rooms to be discovered, rather than solitary fortresses to be attacked.' Whilst theology is talk about God, we must recognize

> that no words, no thoughts, no symbols can encompass the richness of this reality, nor the richness of its disclosure in different lives, communities and traditions. Signs of divine life and grace, of the outpouring of the spirit on earth can be seen in myriad forms in human history and consciousness. From the perspective of *faith*, different world religions can be seen as different gifts of the spirit to humanity. Without losing our respective identities and the precious heritage and roots of our own faith, we can learn to see in a new way the message and insights of our faith in the light of that of others. By

relating our respective visions of the Divine to each other, we can discover a still greater splendour of divine life and grace.

For Christians, the person of Jesus Christ, his life and suffering, his death and resurrection, will always remain the primary source of knowledge and truth about God.

I am not advocating a single-minded, and synthetic model of world religion. Nor was Sir Francis Younghusband. What I want is for each tradition, and especially my own, 'to break through its own particularity', as Paul Tillich put it . . . The way to achieve this, he says, 'is not to relinquish one's religious tradition for the sake of a universal concept which would be nothing but a concept. The way is to penetrate into the depths of one's own religion, in devotion, thought and action. In the depth of every living religion there is a point at which religion itself loses its importance, and that to which it points breaks through its particularity, elevating it to spiritual freedom and to a vision of the spiritual presence in other expressions of the ultimate meaning of man's existence.'[20]

There does not seem to have been a Younghusband Lecture that discussed this issue from a Buddhist point of view, but the Buddhist scholar Ven. Pandith M. Vajiragnana, in his response to Professor Hans Küng at the 1988 WCF conference said: 'Buddhists are not looking for a convergence of religions.' Quoting the well-known edict of the Buddhist Emperor Asoka, Ven. Vajiragnana continued: 'Let us be prepared to accept our crucial differences without trying to throw a threadbare rope between them. Rather let us build bridges of better understanding, tolerance for diverse views, plus encouragement for morality and ethical culture. This is where harmony is to be found.'[21]

It may be seen that whilst all speakers affirm the importance of understanding and mutual respect, their views as to the relationship of religions may differ. To some the mystery of the divine transcends all human language, for others it is shared ethical imperatives that are vital. These differences are reflected in the varying motivation of members of the congress. Indeed they stimulate the continuing debate about the relationship of religions to each other to which WCF has made a significant contribution.

In recent years the subjects have been more varied. In 1990, Indarjit Singh spoke on 'A Sikh Approach to World Peace'. In 1993 the speaker was HE Dr L. Singhvi, a Jain. In 1994, Dr John Taylor, a former secretary-general of the World Conference on Religion and Peace, spoke about efforts at reconciliation in former Yugoslavia. His lecture brought some strong reactions from those who thought that it was too even-handed and did not show sufficient moral indignation about ethnic cleansing.

In 1995, the speaker was Patrick French, author of a recent biography of Younghusband, to which several references have already been made. He spoke about 'Younghusband's Religious Visions'. To mark the sixtieth anniversary, the 1996 lecture on 'How Far Can We Travel Together? Facing the Real Issues of Interfaith Dialogue' will ge given by Dr George Carey, the present Archbishop of Canterbury.

The lectures have all been interesting and significant in themselves, but an added value is that a member of one faith speaks and reflects in the company of those who belong to another faith tradition. Hearing how people interpret and live out their faith today helps us to overcome the barriers not only of ignorance and mistrust but of misunderstanding. The lectures show the need for us to draw on the wisdom of the great spiritual traditions as, in Cantwell Smith's words, we 'jointly construct a common future'.[22]

# 9. 'Truly Extraordinary – Foreign Religions in a Christian Church': interfaith prayer

It has been said that religions meet where religions take their source, in God. The deepest meeting of people of faith is as they wait together in the acknowledged presence of the Eternal Mystery.

The *Church Times* for 19 November 1869 reported that the opening of the Suez Canal had been marked by 'religious services of a somewhat mixed character, Mussulmen and Roman Catholics each taking part in them'.[1] Presumably this refers to separate services, but it is a reminder that there is quite a long history to occasions when people of different religions are together to pray. I have attempted to summarize this history, which certainly dates back to the 1893 World's Parliament of Religions, in the forthcoming book *All in Good Faith*.[2] Here, therefore, I shall concentrate on the World Congress of Faiths' contribution to this development.

In Britain, WCF has pioneered the arrangement of special times for people of different faiths to meet together to pray, as well as providing the opportunity for members to meditate together and to be present at each other's times of prayer.

Occasions when people of different religions pray together have been given a variety of names. They are sometimes called all-faiths services or multifaith worship or interfaith prayer. Sometimes more neutral words such as 'celebration' or 'act of witness' are used. A distinction is sometimes made between 'praying together', which implies joint prayer, and 'being together to pray', which suggests praying in each other's presence but not saying the same prayer together. The latter term suggests rather more clearly that each religion is distinct. These occasions have been held in churches of many denominations, in synagogues, temples and other religious or secular buildings.

At the 1936 World Congress of Faiths, each morning started with prayers led by a member of one faith. As Younghusband explained in a broadcast prior to the Congress: 'Every morning before the proceedings begin there will be held devotional meetings, conducted on one day by a Hindu in the Hindu manner, on another day by a Muslim in the Muslim way and so on. At these all members of the Congress will be welcomed in the hope that they may in some measure catch the spirit of each of the different religions.'[3] The final session included readings from the scriptures of the world. Some hymns were sung during the Congress. All were taken from the Christian tradition but they were chosen in the hope that many members of other faiths also would feel able to sing them.

Similar arrangements were made at the early conferences of the World Congress of Faiths. In this, Sir Francis probably received help from Will Hayes, an early supporter of WCF, who had published in 1924 *A Book of Twelve Services*, which were universalist in character and which expressed Hayes' belief that the religion of the future would be a world religion.[4]

One of the first public services in which members of different religions read from their scriptures was the memorial service for Sir Francis Younghusband. It was almost certainly the first such service to be held in an Anglican church, and took place at St Martin-in-the-Fields on 10 August 1942. Participants included Bhikkhu Thittila, Sir Atul Chatterjee, Rabbi Dr Salzberger and Sir Hassan Suhrawardy. Dorothy Thorold remembered the service as 'truly, truly extraordinary. I had never seen anything like it at that time. It really was most unusual to have foreign religions gathered at that kind of service in a Christian church – but quite appropriate.'[5] The *Church Times*, whilst careful not to speak ill of the dead, made it clear that, in its view, it had been a 'rather improper performance'.[6]

By the early fifties, an all-faiths service had become a regular feature of the World Congress of Faiths' annual conference. Then, in 1953, in response to Queen Elizabeth II's request at the time of her coronation that people of all religions should pray for her, a public service was arranged.[7] Thereafter, for many years, the WCF arranged an annual all-faiths service. Distinguished figures were asked to give the address, including the Indian High Commissioner, Vijaya Lakshmi Pandit, Sir Basil Henriques, Sir

Participants in an early all-faiths service [E. H. Emanuel. Courtesy *The Jewish Chronicle*]

John Glubb, the Hon. Lily Montagu and Dr Edward Carpenter.

In 1958, the service was held for the first time in an Anglican church, St Botolph's, by invitation of George Appleton who at the time was vicar there. The preacher was Dr Aurabinda Basu, a lecturer at Durham University. In 1961, the service was held at St John's Wood Liberal Synagogue. Ten years later it was held for the first time in a Roman Catholic church, at the Church of the Holy Rosary in Marylebone. The preacher was Fr Tom Corbishley who insisted that the service *was* an act of worship. Despite the differences between religions, there was enough in common, he said, to come together in worship. In 1972, for the first time, the preacher was a Muslim, Al Haj Sheik M. Tufail.

The most memorable services perhaps were when the Dalai Lama spoke, once at the West London Synagogue in 1973 and again at Bloomsbury Central Baptist Church in 1981. The latter service was held on a hot summer evening and the church was packed. At the start everyone was asked to offer his or her neighbour a greeting of peace. This created a relaxed and happy atmosphere. In his sermon, the Dalai Lama said he disliked formality. Neither birth nor death were formal! He said we needed variety of religions, just as we like variety of foods. Each has a particular insight to share.

In recent years, whilst WCF has continued to arrange times for meditation and prayer at its various conferences, the tradition of an annual all-faiths service has not been maintained. Occasional public services have been organized, for example at the end of the Year of Inter-religious Understanding and Co-operation, but it has been felt that a number of such services are now arranged in different parts of the country, so that a big central service is less necessary.

## A matter of controversy

In the mid sixties the question of 'interfaith worship' became a matter of controversy. In 1965 a 'Ceremony of Religious Affirmation' was arranged at St Mary-le-Bow by the Revd Joseph McCulloch, a member of WCF, to mark the opening of the Commonwealth Arts Festival. The event, attended by Prince Philip, included readings offered by representatives of each of the great world religions. The following year, the first Commonwealth Day multifaith celebration, attended by the Queen, was held at St Martin-in-the-Fields.

The next year, some Christians, led by the Revd Christopher Wansey, objected to the Commonwealth Day service and also to the WCF annual conference service held at Great St Mary's Church, Cambridge. The Bishop of Ely allowed the service to proceed and, in the event, only a handful of protesters gathered outside the church, although correspondence about it continued in the church press for several weeks.

In his sermon, Canon Hugh Montefiore, rector of Great St Mary's who later became Bishop of Birmingham, explained the significance of the service. He suggested there are four stages in our meeting with people of other faiths. First, there is learning about what they believe. Then, there is reflection about what this new knowledge means to us. Then comes the confrontation, when we are stripped naked and grapple with each other in our agreements and disagreements. Then, 'beyond doctrines and

Canon (now Bishop) Hugh Montefiore with Bramchari Binode and Pam
Wylam  [Courtesy *Cambridge Evening News*]

convictions, we move into the reality of God Himself'. We retain
our religious identity.

> We simply acknowledge that we are all creatures of the one
> God, his Spirit is in us all, we all experience the one God, that
> all our lives are lived in him. As our different prayers and
> scriptures in this service witness, we experience before him
> human sinfulness and awe: we offer to him human
> thanksgiving and gratitude: we place before him human desires
> and hopes: we receive from him all that is good and beautiful
> and true. To deny the propriety of common worship seems to
> me almost a blasphemy against the One God who made us all,
> and it is certainly a denial of our common humanity.[8]

The question of interfaith services was taken up by the British
Council of Churches, which in 1968 agreed that churches should
'scrupulously avoid those forms of interfaith worship which
compromise the distinctive faiths of the participants and should

ensure that Christian witness is neither distorted nor muted'.[9] The final draft had read 'all forms of interfaith worship', but this was changed to 'those forms of interfaith worship', after representations from the World Congress of Faiths.

The final report to the British Council of Churches made clear that Christians would not wish to compromise the uniqueness of Christ and that members of other faiths would not wish to compromise their convictions: 'The presupposition of any interfaith service must be the acknowledgement of our religious diversity rather than a presumption of some (lowest) common denominator . . . What needs to be stressed is the religious approach to life and the common endeavour to bring spiritual values to bear on all its aspects.' The report suggested exchange visits to different places of worship and 'occasions on which those of different faiths do in turn what is characteristic of their own religion, enabling the others present to share to the extent to which they conscientiously can'. The latter suggestion seems to be the genesis of what have become known as 'serial interfaith occasions', when members of different faiths in turn offer prayers on a chosen theme.[10]

The World Congress publicly welcomed the British Council of Churches' recognition of the changed situation in Britain. The WCF statement then pointed out that WCF was careful in its services to ensure the 'distinctive witness of all participants'. The statement added that many of those attending interfaith services experienced a new awareness of God and found that their own particular faith had been enriched by contact with other faiths.[11]

In view of the public debate, WCF asked a working group, chaired by Dr Edward Carpenter, to prepare a justification for the services it arranged. As the debate was between Christians, the WCF report, *Inter-Faith Worship*, was drawn up by Christians sympathetic to interfaith activity and was primarily addressed to Christians.

After giving a history of interfaith services and of the then current debate, the report set out the arguments in favour of such services. The first was that all religions worship the same God. This was a view voiced by Bishop George Appleton at a WCF service when he said: 'We stand in worship before the mystery of the final reality to whom or to which we give differing names, so great and deep and eternal that we can never fully understand or grasp the mystery of His Being.'[12] Secondly, it was said that God is the creator of all people and that such services affirmed our common God-given humanity. The difficulty for some of reference to God was acknowledged. The report also noted the ethical values that were shared by members of the great religions and said that an interfaith service could be an occasion of commitment to common action.

The objections of some Christians to interfaith prayer were noted and discussed. The report also reflected the opinions of some members of other faiths, who mostly showed a preference for members of one faith visiting another place of worship rather than for all trying to arrange a joint service. The report included some practical advice and reproduced the texts of some services, including a particularly imaginative one arranged with the help of Donald Swann for the 1972 WCF conference.[13]

The question of whether people of different faiths should occasionally pray together has continued to be a subject of controversy. Reports have been produced by the Archbishops' Consultants on Interfaith Relations (1980), the Committee for Relations with People of Other Faith of the British Council of Churches (1983) and the Inter-Faith Consultative Group of the Church of England's Board of Mission (1992). I was a member of the first two groups and submitted material to the third, of which Alan Race, an active member of WCF and editor of *World Faiths Encounter*, was a member. Whilst some Christians still strongly oppose interfaith prayer, many more have come to see that it is appropriate on special occasions and the practice has become quite widespread.[14]

Many members of WCF take part in the annual Week of Prayer for World Peace, founded in 1974, partly on the initiative of George Appleton and Edward Carpenter. For many years, Canon Gordon Wilson, who sat on the WCF executive for some time, was the organizing secretary. He has been succeeded by Jonathan Blake. In the mid eighties, as many as 100,000 leaflets were printed.[15]

Recently, WCF has given renewed attention to the question of interfaith prayer. A multifaith working party has been set up, which has consulted widely. The opinions of many local interfaith groups and relevant organizations have been sought. It is intended to publish a resource book on multifaith prayer, *All in Good Faith*. Whereas most previous publications on this subject have been by Christians, for this WCF book on multifaith prayer, members of different faiths have been asked to share their views in the context of their religion's understanding of prayer, worship or meditation. The texts to be included in the anthology have been chosen by members of different religious communities.

The book is planned to be in four sections. The first will give some history of the development of interfaith services and of the discussion about them, followed by a series of chapters in which members of different faiths explain a little about their religion's view of prayer or worship or meditation and the attitude of members of that religion to interfaith prayer. The second part of the book will be an anthology of texts on twelve chosen themes. The third part will reproduce some orders of service and the fourth part will include an annotated bibliography of collections of readings and prayers.

To broaden the consultation, a weekend conference was arranged at Ammerdown in November 1994 on multifaith worship, at which Shahin Bekhradnia, a Zoroastrian, Swami Tripurananda, Rabbi Rachel Montagu and I spoke. Anula Beckett, adviser for inter-religious affairs for the Diocese of Bristol, said in her report of the conference that 'the first Multi-Faith meeting I was closely involved with was an interfaith "service" at Bristol Cathedral, in the Chapter House, in 1988. It was a joyful and moving occasion, but I little knew how much trouble it would cause.' This was because some Anglicans threatened to take legal action against an interfaith service being held in a building dedicated to the worship of the Holy Trinity. The weekend, she said, 'affirmed that we should continue our efforts to pursue greater inter-religious understanding through "Interfaith Celebrations"'.[16]

The conference also affirmed the need for great care and sensitivity in the arrangement of interfaith times of prayer and that they are special events, not  replacements for the regular patterns of worship of any one faith community.

Interfaith times of prayer are likely to remain controversial just because they challenge the exclusiveness of some faith communities. At the same time, they can be a deeply moving experience of the unity to be discovered in the presence of the divine – a pointer to what Younghusband called 'the underlying and overarching harmony which may reconcile all people of faith'.[17]

# 10. 'Pages Enriched by Lives Dedicated to Truth': publications

## The journal

Through its journal WCF has sought to disseminate the lectures and conference papers to a wider audience. The aim has been to address a non-specialist serious readership, helping them to learn about the religions of the world and to consider how the relationship between them can be more creative and harmonious.

During the Second World War, Sir Francis Younghusband himself, as we have seen, started a chairman's circular letter, which was continued by Baron Palmstierna. It was designed to maintain contact between the scattered members of WCF. By 1941, this had developed from a typewritten sheet to a four-page printed pamphlet.

In 1949, Sir John Stewart-Wallace persuaded a young member, Heather McConnell, who had just returned from the Far East, to launch a journal for the WCF. 'My briefing', she recalled, 'was not to be academic and above the heads of our readers but neither was it to play to the lowest common denominator. It should strive to be of general interest to our members in many parts of the world. "Always remember", said Baron Palmstierna, "that we are a *movement* and not a study group."'[1] The journal was named *Forum* and sold for 6d, the equivalent of 2½p. It soon became a journal with reprinted talks, commissioned articles and extensive book reviews. The editor's notes gave news of WCF activities.

Until his death, Baron Palmstierna contributed a regular, inspirational column. His last letter, written shortly before his death, ended with these words: 'Within each human soul exists a link with life eternal which gives us certainty of individual immortality. Death is evidently nothing but the opening in the wall which makes it possible for religious life to continue to progress independently and move ahead on the other side of the wall.'[2]

In 1961 the journal was renamed *World Faiths*, 'as more

descriptive of the contents'.[3] Heather McConnell, who gave a lifetime of service to WCF, continued as editor until 1976.

Looking back, with a hundred issues of the periodical lying on her table, Heather McConnell wrote of the way in which the journal had linked countless friends across the world. The correspondence she received showed that the journal was passed from hand to hand. She recalled some of the distinguished contributors who had submitted material – Sir John Glubb, Professor Geoffrey Parrinder, Professor Norman Bentwich, Christmas Humphreys, Marco Pallis, to name but a few. She remembered some of the important events in the life of the Congress which had been recorded – conferences in Paris and Holland, the opening of Younghusband House, the Dalai Lama's visit. 'Most of all,' she concluded, 'the pages are enriched by the personalities of those who made it all happen, by the many whose lives were dedicated to Truth and understanding and to building bridges of interfaith unity. To have had the privilege of their friendship and of drawing on their wisdom has been the most worthwhile experience of my life.'[4]

In 1976, I succeeded Heather McConnell as editor. There was a lot of work, checking the proofs, pasting up the pages, trying to ensure that the journal was on time and that it remained solvent. Heather said that one compositor always added a 't' whenever the word 'rabbi' appeared in the text. The material, however, was always fascinating and it was a privilege to be in touch with many inspiring people across the world. 'The editor', as Heather wrote, 'is simply the conductor of an orchestra and it is due to the many "players" involved that the concert has continued unbroken.'[5]

The main regret is that so few took advantage of the rich and varied diet. Looking at *World Faiths* No. 100 – the first issue that I edited in 1976 – there is a fascinating article by Kenneth Leech, known for books such as *Soul Friend* and *The Social God*, on 'Youth's Demand for Change': 'Whether the mass of young people become more conformist, more quiescent, more compromised, or whether they become more critical, more visionary, more athirst for justice, one thing is certain,' he warned, 'they will not be deceived by a superficial tampering with the surface manifestations of religious life.' He suggested that it will be from the Christians of the Third World that the Churches in the West would be 'recalled to the realities of prophecy and vision'.[6] The issue includes a sensitive account by W. W. Simpson, secretary of the International Council of Christians and Jews, of the first conference to be held by the ICCJ in Jerusalem; a comment on the Festival of Islam by Sir John Lawrence, editor for many years of *Frontier*, and an incisive report by Dr Stanley Samartha, an Indian theologian who was director of the World Council of Churches programme on Dialogue with People of Living Faiths and Ideologies, on the debate about dialogue at the 1975 Nairobi Assembly of the World Council of Churches.

After some negotiation, in 1980 it was agreed to unite the WCF journal with the journal *Insight*, which had been produced from 1976 by the Temple of Understanding. The merged journal was called *World Faiths Insight*. Professor Seshagiri Rao and I became co-editors. Seshagiri Rao, who graduated from Mysore University, studied at the Center for the Study of World Religions at Harvard University. He subsequently became Professor of Religious Studies at the University of Virginia in Charlottesville. He has written extensively, especially in the field of Gandhian studies, and is now editing a multi-volume encyclopaedia of Hinduism.

The happy co-operation between a Hindu professor and an Anglican clergyman itself symbolized the spirit of WCF. The link increased the breadth of contributions and gave an international flavour to the journal. The American market was likely to be in universities that offered courses in the study of religions, whereas the British readership was less academic. This added to the considerations in ensuring the right balance of articles – considerations which included fair representation of different religions and countries, as well as a proper gender balance. Another difficulty was that it was inappropriate for an international journal to carry information of interest only to WCF members, such as news of British local interfaith groups. This difficulty was met by producing a British supplement, which was to be the seed of *Interfaith News*. A further difficulty was the constant struggle to break even, as *World Faiths Insight* never received a subsidy.

The journal carried, besides a variety of articles, news of

The Revd Alan Race with Irene Chapman of Leicester Liberal Synagogue

major interfaith conferences and events as well as book reviews. Although the circulation is still not large, the journal goes to many parts of the world – often to libraries. It has been one of the ways by which WCF has tried to offer a service to the world rather than just to Britain.

In 1991, the Revd Alan Race, an Anglican clergyman particularly known for his book *Christians and Religious Pluralism*, succeeded me as editor. Alan Race was born in Stockton-on-Tees in 1951. His initial training was in chemistry, but he followed this with theological studies at Oxford and Birmingham. He was ordained in the Church of England in 1976. His interest in interfaith encounter grew out of living in multicultural and multifaith Bradford in the early seventies. Dr George Chryssides, a lecturer in religious studies, became review editor.

Although Professor Seshagiri Rao has continued as co-editor, the Temple of Understanding decided, in 1991, that they were unable to continue their support for the journal. Despite this, a significant North American readership has been maintained.

Together with the change of editor, other changes were introduced. The first was a change of name to *World Faiths Encounter* (March 1992). This was to indicate that the revised journal intended to focus 'more sharply on both the interactions between religious traditions and on the relationships between people of different religious communities, in our contemporary world'. This reflected the growing recognition that the meeting of religions had an important impact on society – for good or bad. 'We live with competing religious convictions pervading every department of life.' The journal was designed to appeal to many different constituencies – 'theologians and religious specialists of the different traditions, educationalists, inter-faith organizations and local activists who are faced with the daily confusions and joys which a pluralist society generates'.[7] Such a wide audience creates difficulties, but these have been successfully met and the great variety of content indicates the range of contemporary inter-religious encounter.

The format and layout of the journal was redesigned to produce a more attractive publication – together with an eye-catching logo and green cover.

## Interfaith News

In the early eighties, WCF approached other bodies to discuss the publication of a news-sheet of interfaith activities, to keep pace with the proliferation of interfaith activities in Britain. The Committee for Relations with People of Other Faiths of the British Council of Churches, the Interfaith Association, the Week of Prayer for World Peace, the World Conference of Religions for Peace (UK) and the World Congress of Faiths agreed to sponsor a publication, which was called *Interfaith News*. By the late eighties, the Interfaith Association had merged with WCF, but its place as a co-sponsor was soon taken by the then recently established Inter Faith Network. The first issue of the news-sheet appeared in 1982.

The first editor of *Interfaith News* was Geoffrey Bould, a member of the Society of Friends, who has had a particular concern for prisoners of conscience. He was succeeded in 1989 by Dr Paul Weller, who at that time was resources officer of the Inter Faith Network and who now heads the Religious Resource and Research Centre at the University of Derby. The organizing committee was chaired by Brian Pearce and the administrative work was handled by WCF.

*Interfaith News* gave a lively account of activities, advertised future events and helped to ensure that those working in this field, for various national and local organizations, kept in touch with each other. To glance through the copies of *Interfaith News* is to be reminded of the significant events of the eighties, which was an important decade in the development of interfaith work not only in Britain, but across the world. No. 3 has the headline 'Interfaith Breakthrough?' with a report of interfaith activities at the sixth assembly of the World Council of Churches, held in Vancouver in 1982. At the assembly, for the first time, members of other faiths addressed a plenary session, whereas twenty years before, at the New Delhi assembly, people of other faiths could not even attend as accredited press representatives.[8]

Issue No. 12 highlights Archbishop Robert Runcie's Younghusband Lecture, which Dr Kenneth Cracknell, then secretary of the British Council of Churches' Committee for Relations with People of Other Faiths, wrote of as a 'miracle at Lambeth Palace':

The miracle for those with hearts and minds to discern it was in this: Dr Runcie was introduced at the beginning of the lecture by a Muslim Sheikh and thanked at its close by a Rabbi. Both spoke warmly and affectionately of the

Archbishop . . . It was a splendid occasion, but more than that, it was a marvel, a portent, a miracle of God for those with eyes to see . . . Thank God for Dr Runcie, and thank God for Sheikh Gamal and Rabbi Hugo Gryn and for so many others who sing the dawn chorus of a new creation.[9]

The next issue spoke of the historic World Day of Prayer for Peace at Assisi in October 1986. Next year, *Interfaith News* heralded the 'Birth of the Inter Faith Network'. The June 1988 issue, reporting on the Global Forum of Spiritual and Political Leaders, held in Oxford, is headlined 'Towards a Global Ethic' – pointing forward to the work of the Parliament of the World's Religions in Chicago five years later.

The issues of the early nineties reflect a changing scene. The optimism of the eighties was giving way to awareness that religious passion was still a divisive force. The June 1990 edition concentrated on some of the issues raised by the publication of Salman Rushdie's *The Satanic Verses* and included a report of the refusal to extend the blasphemy laws. The February 1991 issue highlighted Dr Runcie's address to the Inter Faith Network. After talking about the progress in interfaith relations, he spoke of the hostility to other faiths still evident in some parts of the Churches and of what he called 'the tribalising of religion' in places as varied as Sri Lanka, India and Northern Ireland as well as the rise of Islamic 'fundamentalism'.[10]

It is difficult to ensure that a newsletter breaks even. The cost of postage and administration makes an economic price unrealistic in terms of expecting people to pay for it. The subscription rate of £1 and then £1.50 for three copies never fully covered costs and in 1991 *Interfaith News*, for financial reasons, had to cease publication.

## One Family

The wish to link the various activities up and down Britain during the Year of Inter-religious Understanding and Co-operation in 1993 led to the production of a fresh newsletter. *One Family*, collated and edited by Sandy Martin and Jean Potter, was produced to list the various activities of the year.

*One Family* has been found to be so useful that it has continued to appear three times a year. It is published by the World Congress of Faiths and reports on WCF events and gives details of future programmes. It is not, however, confined to news of WCF but includes details of the activities and programmes of quite a number of interfaith organizations in Great Britain.

## Other publications

WCF has sponsored a number of other publications. The papers of the pre-war conferences were published.[11]

Two booklets have told the history of WCF. In 1956 Arthur Peacock wrote *Fellowship through Religion*, which gives a good summary of the early years.[12] In 1976, for the fortieth anniversary, I wrote a brief account of WCF's life and work. Bishop George Appleton wrote a foreword (a printer's error called it 'A Forward', which perhaps expressed the hopes of the moment!) in which he included his personal 'guidelines', which had emerged after nearly fifty years of contact with people of other faiths. They are the principles that guided a Christian who was committed to building good interfaith relations, but ones that, suitably adapted, he hoped members of other faiths could make their own. They are still well worth reproducing:

1. Be deeply interested in the religious experience of people of other Faiths, the faith they have formulated from it and the values by which they live.
2. Pay special attention to the central faith or gospel of each religion and examine its relevance to others.
3. Look keenly to see in what ways God may be at work in other religions, for in my own faith he is Creator of all men, the Source of all truth, goodness and love.
4. Be ready to receive new truth, which will verify, correct and enlarge what I have already received.
5. Judge other religions by the highest in them and not by failures or distortions, and hope that their adherents will reciprocate in reference to my expression of Christianity.
6. Be as true as grace and my own effort can make me to the mind and standards of Jesus Christ, and want others to live up

to the highest they know from their own religion.

7. Work with others to discover the principles of true religion in our contemporary world.

8. Not to proselytise, but be ready to accept transfer either way if a person feels he can serve God and men better by a change in religious affiliation.

9. Be eager to meet people of other Faiths within our own neighbourhood, welcome the expression of their own self-understanding, and work with them for social justice, human happiness and human unity.

10. Make love the mainspring of my life, realising that a wide open-heart and a great love always opens the hearts of others.

11. Make reciprocity the principle for inter-religious thinking and relationships, allowing to others the same right to commitment, witness and proclamation as I claim for myself.

12. Not to be over-defensive of my Lord Jesus Christ, always bearing in mind the humility of the birth at Bethlehem, the defencelessness of the Cross on Calvary and the glory of the Resurrection.[13]

Other WCF publications include some of the Younghusband Lectures, which have been published as pamphlets. WCF also arranged, as we have seen, for the publication of the report on *Interfaith Worship* by Galliards, part of Stainer & Bell. Further, as already mentioned, a resource book on multifaith prayer, *All in Good Faith*, is being prepared for publication.

# 11. *From Aids to yoga: working with others*

The files in the WCF archives at the Parkes library at Southampton University cover a wide range of subjects. More than half relate to correspondence with other organizations. The list includes the anti-apartheid movement; 'Black People in Britain: The Way Forward', the title of a conference in the seventies; humanism; the Niwano Peace Prize; religious dance; the Teilhard Centre for the Future of Man; Ways of the Spirit, a spiritual festival held in London in the seventies; the World Peace Prayer Society, and many more.

Many organizations have in the past approached the World Congress of Faiths to introduce them to faith communities in Britain. Religion touches on so many aspects of life: the arts, health, social issues, the concern for peace, human rights and justice. At the same time, WCF has been in touch with faith communities and corresponds with many religious bodies. As an educational charity, WCF has been concerned to educate people of all ages to appreciate the great religions, so there are letters to educational bodies and to the media. WCF has also tried to encourage contact between people of different faiths not only in different parts of the United Kingdom, but throughout the world, so there is correspondence with both local and international interfaith groups and organizations.

In this chapter, we shall look at WCF's efforts to encourage local interfaith activity in Britain, its support for the Inter Faith Network of the UK, its educational work and its contact with one or two other societies.

## Local interfaith activity

Local interfaith activity has largely depended on the enthusiasm and initiative of one or two keen people in an area. Some of these have been members of the WCF and in a history of WCF it is appropriate to concentrate on these people. This is not, however, the place to tell the varied and fascinating story of the development of local interfaith activity, which now exists in many parts of

Britain. That history deserves to be written and will tell of many more far-seeing, generous and creative people.

## Kathleen de Beaumont

Thanks particularly to the inspiration of the Hon. Mrs de Beaumont, there was a lively branch of WCF in Cambridge in the fifties. Kathleen de Beaumont, the eldest child of Lord and Lady O'Hagan, was born in London in 1876. She was brought up a Roman Catholic, but when she was a teenager, the family converted to the Church of England. This caused a rift with many of the relations which took many years to heal. Kathleen was a devout Anglo-Catholic but of broad vision. She acclaimed the writings of Teilhard de Chardin and the ecumenical outlook of Pope John XXII.[1] Her husband, known as Dr Klein until the time of their marriage, had also left the Roman Catholic Church. Soon after they were married, he became the Unitarian minister at Little Portland Street, Marylebone, in succession to Dr James Martineau, whose writings had greatly influenced Klein.

In 1915, the de Beaumonts moved to Cambridge, where Kathleen was involved in many community activities, especially in work for the Girl Guides. In 1909, she and her two daughters, complete with broomsticks, had attended the first Scout rally at Crystal Palace. Noticing the girls' presence, Sir Robert Baden-Powell enquired about them and decided something must be done for girls. Once it was decided to set up the Girl Guides, Baden-Powell asked Mrs de Beaumont to become County Commissioner for Cambridgeshire, a position that she held for thirty years. In Cambridge, she and her husband made many friends, especially Dr Raven, Master of Christ's College, and Dr Burkitt, Professor of Theology.

Kathleen's husband died in 1934. Soon afterwards, she met Sir Francis Younghusband and took part in the founding of WCF, which, she wrote, 'became a major interest and activity in my life'.[2] Unfortunately, her memoirs give few details of her work for WCF. During the war she was active in her support for *La France Libre*. In 1953, she returned to London, after forty years in Cambridge.

Back in London, Kathleen regularly attended WCF meetings,

serving on the executive committee and becoming a vice-president. She also participated regularly in the contemplative meditation meetings arranged by the Revd R. G. Coulson, mentioned in chapter 5. For many years she suffered from arthritis and her last years were ones of illness, but her spirit was indomitable:

> Finally, came illness – a truly blessed experience because at the same time that I was stricken by the illness which kept me house-bound for years, some of the works of Pere Teilhard de Chardin came into my hands. A new heaven opened for me with the vision glorious of the Cosmic Christ. To have lived to witness this opening of a new era in the history of religion on this earth is indeed a privilege for which I am humbly thankful.[3]

Kathleen de Beaumont, like Sir Francis Younghusband, had deep personal spiritual experiences and a wide sympathy for the faiths of the world. She was also a member of the Fellowship of Meditation and was much influenced by Marion Dunlop. With her links with and deep concern for France, she helped to maintain links with the *Union des Croyants* (the French branch of WCF) and became a close friend of Comtesse Jacques de Pange.

It was Kathleen de Beaumont who in the early fifties inspired the Cambridge branch of WCF in which both Canon Raven and Dr Stewart Carter, the Unitarian minister, took an active interest. The branch had a varied programme and attracted good support. In 1954, for example, the *Cambridge Daily News* reported that there had been a crowded service for people of all faiths.[4]

### Lady Madeline Lees and George Harrison

During the fifties, a WCF branch was established at Bournemouth and Poole, and several events took place at the home of Lady Madeline Lees at Lytchett in Dorset. A film was made to promote the idea of 'World Peace through Religious Drama'.[5] Lady Lees remained a supporter of WCF throughout her life and continued, almost to the end, to paint watercolour cards to raise money for the cause.

Another 'devotee' of Younghusband was George Harrison,

who himself had had deep mystical experiences. For a time he was the WCF's north of England officer, but there seem to have been disagreements about the financial arrangements for his work. Nevertheless, despite the demands of his work for British Rail, he found time to do much to promote WCF in the north of England. There are many reports in *World Faiths* of talks that he gave and of all-faiths services being held in Sheffield and Leeds and other northern cities.

## Bristol and Bath

The beginnings of interfaith work in the Bristol and Bath area owe a lot to two very remarkable, if very different, people: Albert Polack and Brian Pamplin.

In the late sixties a 'Younghusband branch of WCF' was established in the Bristol and Bath area. At the time, I was a visiting lecturer at Bristol University. I met Albert Polack and we talked about Younghusband.

Albert's father, the Revd Joseph Polack, was the first housemaster of Polack's House, a house for Jewish boys at Clifton College. Albert was a schoolboy there and in 1926 himself became housemaster of Polack's House. He knew about and admired Clifton's famous son, Francis Younghusband. When he 'retired' in 1949, he became education officer of the Council of Christians and Jews. By the late sixties, he had just 'retired' again and had returned to live in Bristol. Together we arranged a meeting, at which it was agreed to set up a Bristol branch of WCF. Albert suggested that as Sir Francis had been a pupil at Clifton College, it should be called the Younghusband Branch. Tony Reese, a member of the Bristol Progressive Synagogue, soon became an active member and officer of the branch and is still active in interfaith work in Bristol.

After a time, Dr Brian Pamplin, a science lecturer at Bath University, became interested, partly through his study of the writings of Teilhard de Chardin. He decided to set up a new group, called SHARIFH, Sharing the Future in Hope. This was designed to seek reconciliation between the religions and science. The work was centred on Bath University and there were several interfaith gatherings at the chaplaincy centre. He is still commemorated in

Albert Polack [Alfred F. Carpenter]

Bath by the Pamplin Addresses, which seek to promote dialogue both between members of different religions and between them and scientists. Although SHARIFH was potentially a national and international group, it remained centred in Bath. After Brian's death, those in the group whose main interest was interfaith dialogue and those more interested in Brian's scientific and spiritual enquiries separated, and two independent groups were established. The Bath interfaith group has continued to have a regular and varied programme. The difficulty is that faith communities other than Christian are small and it is hard to get a balanced membership – not that more than a few Christians have been actively interested.

In Bristol, by contrast, many faith communities are well established. There is an active interfaith group in the city, which had a particularly imaginative programme during the Year of Inter-religious Understanding and Co-operation. Neither the Bath nor Bristol interfaith group is now a 'branch' of WCF, but several members of both groups are members of WCF.

Brian Pamplin gradually moved to a universalist position. He saw God's presence in every form of religion and indeed in all life.

In 1983, he spent Christmas at the ashram of Sai Baba and heard him preach about Jesus. From that sermon he took the words that became SHARIFH's motto: 'There is one religion – the Religion of Love.' He sought not only the reconciliation of religions but of science and religion at the highest philosophical level. He was deeply interested in the relationship of the latest scientific thought to the speculations of Buddhist metaphysicians. This search for reconciliation was not just an intellectual matter, but for the future of the world and for the sake of the poor. From service in Korea, he was personally aware of the horrors of modern warfare. Just before his death he had visited Mother Teresa who had directed his attention forcefully to the needs of the destitute.[6]

## Bill and Joan Steiner

Another person who combined an interest in the reconciliation of religions and of religion and science was Bill Steiner, a Unitarian who served for many years on the WCF executive. He regularly taped the lectures given at WCF conferences and the tapes are still a rich source of inspiration. He and his wife, Joan, came on several WCF tours. Joan, an Anglican, herself gave her energies to work for WCF in Wellingborough, where an active WCF branch existed for many years.

The above groups were all initially established as WCF branches. After a time, it became clear that less formal links were more helpful.

There are today many other local interfaith groups. In some, members of WCF have played an active part. In Wolverhampton, for example, there has for many years been a well-organized and lively group, in which a leading member, Ivy Gutridge, has long been a member of WCF. In Glasgow, the moving spirit was a deaconess of the Church of Scotland, the late Stella Reekie, who became a keen supporter of WCF. Her home at the International Flat became the venue for numerous arranged and chance interfaith meetings. Stella helped to establish the Sharing of Faiths group in the city, where there have been regular exhibitions and where the St Mungo Museum was opened in 1993. The aims of the Sharing of Faiths group, which reflect Stella's wide concerns, are worth recording. They are:

- to share human friendship across religious boundaries
- to foster understanding among people of different races and faiths
- to learn from each other
- to share religious experience
- to deepen our religious insights.[7]

The stories of other groups, such as Westminster Interfaith or Leeds Concord, also deserve to be told and mention made of the many people, such as Penny Reynolds of Bognor, who by their gift of friendship have brought people together. Groups are very different, just as the needs and characters of towns and cities up and down the country vary. Some are very practical in their programmes, some more philosophical in their discussions. Some are well organized, some quite informal, some are universalist in outlook, some are more akin to religious community relations councils where the distinctive identity of each faith community is clear.

Local interfaith groups have offered people a chance to meet their neighbours who belong to other faith communities. Such meeting has broken down ignorance and prejudice and has led to friendships, which have enriched many lives. Local groups have dealt with a wide range of enquiries, but most important they have helped to sustain and build up the fabric of the multifaith, multicultural and multiethnic society that Britain is becoming.

## The Interfaith Network for the UK

How to give some cohesion to this varied activity has been a continuing concern. There has also been a wish to ensure that national interfaith organizations should work as partners.

In 1965, besides WCF, only the Council of Christians and Jews and the London Society for Jews and Christians were already active. Since then, all three organizations have expanded their work and influence. Whilst Christian–Jewish dialogue retains its specific character, it has become more related to wider interfaith dialogue. In 1977, the British Council of Churches Committee for

Relations with People of Other Faiths was formed, with the Revd Kenneth Cracknell as the first full-time secretary, followed by the Revd Dr Clinton Bennett. The work has now been taken on by the Council of Churches of Britain and Ireland, with Canon Dr Christopher Lamb as officer for interfaith relations. Several denominations now have special committees for interfaith reflection and dialogue, some with at least part-time officers. Meanwhile, other faith communities have developed national structures. There is, for example, a National Council of Hindu Temples and an Imams and Mosques Council.

There has also been a growing interest in the teaching of world religions. Compared to twenty years ago, there is a plethora of interfaith activity and meetings and greater support from the leaders of the different faith communities. Some indication of the variety of religious life in Britain and of the various bodies linking faith communities is given in *Religions in the UK: A Multi-Faith Directory*, edited by Paul Weller of the University of Derby, which runs to over 600 pages.[8] Even so, those involved need to be aware that a large majority of the population are still untouched by these developments.

In 1977–8, Canon Peter Schneider, the Revd Jack Austin and I, with some others, made tentative moves to explore forming a 'Consultative Interfaith Council'. In a memorandum, Canon Schneider outlined the possibilities. On the projected council, compared to the BCC Committee on Relations with People of Other Faiths, 'members of various Faith Communities would meet and discuss as equal partners. All are hosts and none are guests.' Compared to WCF, which was based on individual enthusiasts, the Council 'would consciously relate to the various Faith Communities as a whole and seek to provide a structured forum of meeting and discussion':

The aims of this Council can be seen as facilitating a more comprehensive meeting and acquaintance and knowledge of different Faiths than is at present the case. Further its purpose would be that issues of common interest and concern could be discussed and if it seemed proper decisions reached. In times of crisis the Council would be the obvious framework for urgent consultation and possible united decision, provided this had the support of the Faith Communities represented in the Council.[9]

Nothing came of these moves, partly because of the untimely death of Peter Schneider and because of lack of support from the religious communities.

Some ten years later, Brian Pearce, an active member of WCF, then on leave of absence from the Civil Service, patiently researched the best ways to strengthen good relationships between the faith communities in Britain. One possibility might have been to try very considerably to strengthen and expand the work of WCF, as the Revd Jack Austin had tried ten years before. It became clear that this would have implied that the faith communities had first to accept the view of the relationship between religions implicit in the approach of WCF. Quite a number of members of each religion might have been uneasy about this. The WCF executive, in April 1985, unanimously agreed to give its support to the attempt to establish a new organization, which would bring together representatives of the faith communities and those already active in promoting good interfaith relations.[10] It would be an organization for organizations and not for individuals and it would be a network, dependent on consensus for any policy decisions.

After a consultative period of nearly two years in all, the Inter Faith Network for the United Kingdom was formally established in 1987 and now links over seventy organizations and groups. These include representative bodies from within the main world religious communities in Britain, such as the Council of Churches for Britain and Ireland, the National Council of Hindu Temples and the Buddhist Society; national interfaith organizations, such as the Council of Christians and Jews and the World Congress of Faiths; local interfaith groups, such as the Wolverhampton Inter-Faith Group and the Leeds Concord Interfaith Society; and study centres and academic bodies concerned with the study of religions and the relationships between them, such as the Community Relations Project of Leeds University and the Religious Education Council. Not all local interfaith groups are, at present, affiliated to the Network, but all of them are invited to the area meetings that the Network arranges.

The constitution sets out the aim of the Network as being 'to advance public knowledge and mutual understanding of the teachings, traditions, and practices of the different faith communities in Britain including an awareness both of their distinctive features and of their common ground and to promote good relations between persons of different religious faiths'. At the inaugural meeting, this resolution was adopted:

> We meet today as children of many traditions, inheritors of shared wisdom and of tragic misunderstandings. We recognise our shared humanity and we respect each other's differences. With the agreed purpose and hope of promoting greater understanding between the members of the different faith communities to which we belong and of encouraging the growth of relationships of respect and trust and mutual enrichment in our life together, we hereby jointly resolve: that the Inter Faith Network for the United Kingdom should now be established.[11]

The Network provides information and advice on interfaith matters and helps put organizations and individuals in touch with the different faith communities at national and local level. It is increasingly consulted by government departments, other public-sector and voluntary bodies, the media and the leaders and members of religious communities. The Inner Cities Religious Council, set up by the Department of the Environment in 1993, for example, included three of the Network's officers in its membership.

The Network has held regular national and regional meetings and has organized seminars on particular issues such as 'The Blasphemy Laws', 'Women and Religion', 'Religious Education and Collective Worship in Schools' and 'Religion on Radio and Television'. It has produced a 'Statement on Inter-Religious Relations' and in 1993, issued a short code of conduct on 'Building Good Relations between People of Different Faiths and Beliefs', as well as a longer document called 'Mission, Dialogue and Inter-Religious Encounter'.

For its first years, the co-chairs of the Network were the Rt. Revd Jim Thompson, then Bishop of Stepney, and Hugo Gryn,

Senior Rabbi of the West London Synagogue. They have been succeeded by Indarjit Singh, editor of the *Sikh Messenger*, and the Rt. Revd Roy Williamson, Bishop of Southwark. The growth of the Network and the high regard in which it is held is to the credit of the director, Brian Pearce, who became its first director following his early retirement from the Civil Service, Dr Harriet Crabtree, its deputy director, and the others who have served as members of its staff. They have patiently gained the trust of the various faith communities involved and helped these communities to trust each other.

In their report for 1994–5, the co-chairs stressed the importance of making multifaith Britain a place of harmony and understanding between religions.

> In many areas of the world inter religious conflict causes great hardship and misery. We must never slacken in our endeavours to make sure that misunderstandings and prejudice do not take root here with tragic consequences for our society. Our individual faith traditions need not be sources of conflict. Practised with integrity, they can offer rich resources for a shared life together based on mutual respect and deeply held values.[12]

## Religious education

Education clearly has an important part to play in ensuring that misunderstandings and prejudice do not take root in British society. Much of WCF's work has been in the area of public education, but at times particular attention has been given to the religious education of the young, both in schools and universities.

The 1944 (Butler) Education Act required religious instruction in all local authority schools together with an act of collective worship. Although provision was made for Jewish children, and opting out was permitted, both the instruction and worship were almost wholly Christian, even though, as we have seen, R. A. Butler, in his address to the WCF, recognized that spiritual values are emphasized in all religions. WCF was one of the first bodies to advocate the teaching of world religions and to express concern about provision for the religious education of children of minority faiths. An article in *World Faiths* in March 1961 said there was a need for an 'Advisory Council for Inter-Faith Understanding in Education', 'on which would be representatives of the teachers' bodies, local education authorities, teachers' training colleges, the churches and such organizations as the WCF and the Council of Christians and Jews'.[13] On more than one occasion, Lord Sorensen raised the matter in Parliament.[14]

In 1965 Bernard Cousins, a Jewish member of the Congress, published a booklet giving examples of his own efforts to introduce world religions into the classroom. 'The study of one faith in isolation,' he wrote, 'with scarcely any reference to the greatness of others, can produce a narrowness of outlook, an arrogance and exclusiveness which give rise to suspicion, contempt and dislike for the unfamiliar.'[15] In the same year, the Revd John Rowland compiled an all-faiths Order of Service for World Children's Day, which was distributed through UNICEF.[16]

In 1969, the Congress convened an education advisory committee. At that time it was thought that a new Education Act was being prepared, so the committee's first task was to draw up a statement, issued in July 1970, about the provision of religious education in local authority schools 'with particular reference to the teaching of world religions and the needs of all children in a plural society'. The committee, on which all major religions were represented, argued that religious education should have a place in schools, primarily on educational grounds.

We believe that religious education should have a continuing place in our schools. The primary reason for this is educational. A knowledge of man's religious history is essential to an understanding of our culture and our fellow beings. The spiritual dimension is a part of human experience and pupils should be given the opportunity to understand and assess religious claims. As people of faith we believe that individuals and society need a spiritual basis. Moral values, too, although they may be independent, are often closely related to religious faith.

In calling for the teaching of other religions, besides Christianity,

Catherine Fletcher with Dr Frank Chandra  [Alfred F. Carpenter]

the group said that what was needed was 'the imaginative sympathy that enables a child to appreciate what living by another faith means to its followers'.[17] The committee suggested that assemblies might sometimes be interfaith in character. Subsequently the committee discussed assemblies in greater detail.[18] The education advisory committee of WCF continued for some years, with Catherine Fletcher, a distinguished educationist, in the chair. For some time it considered the misunderstandings that religious communities have about each other. A number of conferences for teachers were arranged and an essay competition for young people was organized.

As education secretary for the British Council of Churches, John Prickett, a former headmaster, was particularly interested in this area. In July 1972, he arranged through the BCC education department a two-day residential interfaith conference on education at Leicester University. A couple of similar conferences had already been held, sponsored by the National Society, in 1970 and 1971. A follow-up to the Leicester conference was held at Westhill College, Selly Oak, in 1973, sponsored by the extra-mural department of Birmingham University. Participants felt it was important that the work should continue, so a new body was formed called the Standing Conference on Inter-Faith Dialogue in Education (SCIFDE). This fledgeling needed a parent, so WCF agreed to be the sponsoring body. John Prickett, who had retired from the BCC, became the very active secretary and Rabbi Hugo Gryn became chairman. A series of conferences has been held, some of which resulted in publications, including *Marriage and the Family*, *Death* and *Initiation Rites*, all edited by John Prickett. The present conference organizer is Angela Wood. Recent conferences have been on 'Work, Rest and Play', 'Woman' and 'Bridges and Barriers'.[19]

At the same time as the WCF education advisory committee agreed a statement on religious education, it produced a simple guide to resources for those wishing to teach world religions. It is a reminder of how few resources were then available that the guide was only four foolscap pages. At much the same time, Peter Woodward of Borough Road College, Isleworth, produced a slightly larger list of resources. This in time grew into a very comprehensive guide. SHAP now produces an annual journal, *World Religions in Education* and the SHAP calendar, which gives the dates of the major festivals of the main religions. SHAP, which was established after a conference to promote the study of religions, held at Shap in the Lake District in 1969, has arranged regular conferences.[20]

To provide a forum where the variety of people concerned for the future of religious education could meet, a religious education council was formed in 1973.[21] This includes representatives of professional organizations of faith communities and of interfaith organizations. WCF has for several years been represented by Dr Owen Cole, a distinguished educationist. The religious education council has recently tried to ensure that the needs of all faith communities were safeguarded in the 1988 Education Act and in its application.

Members of WCF have been active in all these organizations and some are members of local standing advisory conferences on religious education. Others are RE teachers. Yet despite the considerable success of efforts to broaden the scope of religious education and the wide resources now available, the subject is still given a low priority in many schools and WCF should rightly continue to be concerned that children have an opportunity both to grow in their own faith and to learn to appreciate the faiths of others.

The increasing provision of courses on religious studies in British universities, advocated earlier in this century by the Union for the Study of the Great Religions, has been welcomed by WCF. A number of WCF members are active in the British Association for the Study of Religions.[22] WCF has tried to encourage seminaries, theological colleges and other centres for training rabbis and imams to provide teaching about all the great faiths. The increasing availability of good books for students and of translations of religious texts, for example by the International Sacred Literature Trust,[23] should remove any excuse for ignorance.

## Peace and human rights

Too often religious differences have been a cause of bitterness, which is one reason why education about world religions is important. At the same time, in all religions there is a concern for peace, justice and human welfare.

The World Congress of Faiths has therefore worked closely with many other bodies. For example, Dr Edward Carpenter, president of WCF, for many years chaired the United Nations Association's Religious Advisory Committee, on which a number of members of WCF have served. He, together with Bishop Appleton, helped to initiate the Week of Prayer for World Peace. WCF also supported the 'One Million Minutes for Peace' campaign, organized by members of the Brahma Kumaris World Spiritual University.

The World Congress of Faiths has worked closely over the years with the World Conference on Religions and Peace (WCRP), both internationally and in Britain. The hope of the WCF has always been that its activities would contribute to understanding between peoples and so to peace. The 1995 conference, for example, was on the subject of 'Religions in War and Peace'. WCF, however, has not been a campaigning body on specific issues. WCRP has been more focused on questions of disarmament and development.

Recently, with growing popular concern about the environment, there has been renewed interest in what the religions have to say on the subject, shown for example at the Worldwide Fund for Nature's programme in Assisi in 1986. WCF has been represented at some meetings of the Global Forum on Human Survival and at the Summit on Religion and Conservation.

Whilst Younghusband himself and the pioneers of WCF hoped that religious people could 'awaken and develop a world loyalty', much of the work of the Congress has been preparatory to that, in that it has been necessary to dispel prejudice and build up friendly relations between members of different faith communities before they could begin to act together. The programme of the Inter Faith Network and WCF's co-operation with a wide range of other bodies concerned for justice, peace, human rights and the protection of the environment suggests that a new stage in interfaith work is just beginning, not only in Britain but across the world.

# 12. A year of inter-religious understanding and co-operation: 1993 in Britain

## Creating interest

1993 marked the centenary of the World's Parliament of Religions, held in Chicago. The international interfaith organizations, as we shall see, agreed to designate 1993 as 'a Year of Inter-religious Understanding and Co-operation'. In Britain, celebration of the Year was co-ordinated by the World Congress of Faiths.

To prepare for the Year, the World Congress of Faiths called together a small group to discuss how to promote it in Britain. The WCF offered to co-ordinate the activities, but in a way that encouraged as many other groups as possible to arrange a special event to mark the centenary. It was clear that there were not the resources to organize many central events. In fact, the only central events were the launch at Global Co-operation House in January and a concluding service at the West London Synagogue.

First, however, people had to be made aware of the Year. The aim was never just to mark the centenary of the 1893 World's Parliament of Religions at Chicago. We wished rather to focus on the achievements of one hundred years of interfaith activity and to encourage people to look forward to the task ahead.

To many, it was a surprise to learn that the interfaith movement was a hundred years old. They knew little about interfaith work, less about the interfaith organizations and nothing about the World's Parliament of Religions. If we were to gain support for the Year, we had to increase awareness of interfaith activities. My history of the interfaith movement, *Pilgrimage of Hope*, published in February 1992 in Britain and the USA, provided a solid historical account of what had happened and had been achieved.[1] It was deliberately written in a factual rather than a hortatory style. In many faith communities, there is still suspicion of interfaith activity. I wanted to avoid the accusation of special pleading. The aim was to present evidence of what had actually happened, leaving people free to make their own evaluation.

Because there was so much material, the book was long. This meant that it was published as a hardback and so seemed expensive. Something much simpler was also needed, so I prepared a study guide as part of a study pack put together by a small group.[2] Both became quite popular and – a rare event in WCF history – the project made a profit, thanks to much voluntary labour.

We could not, however, rely just upon our own publications. Considerable efforts were made to get news of the Year into a range of journals and newsletters. An enormous variety of publications emanates from religious communities and although, by themselves, they have quite small circulations, they have a significant cumulative effect. The Revd James Paterson was particularly effective at getting the Scottish religious press involved. Local papers reported local events arranged for the Year.

There was some attention in the national media. The launch was featured on BBC Radio's *Thought for the Day*. *The Independent* had a series on inter-religious relations and Indarjit Singh, in particular, mentioned the Year, hoping that it would lead to 'action for a saner world order'.[3] In the autumn of 1993, BBC 1 showed an excellent series called *Faith to Faith*. The first programme, shown as the Chicago Parliament ended, focused on that event. Subsequent programmes looked at the contemporary multifaith situation in Britain. In one, a Christian/Hindu couple talked about the early years of their marriage. In another a group of friends attended worship in a gurdwara, a synagogue and a mosque, and discussed the possibility of people of different faiths worshipping together. Another considered the extent to which the environment is a religious issue. There was some coverage on the radio, including two very thoughtful programmes on the BBC World Service.

Media coverage – both mass and mini media – served to increase public awareness of the possibility of religious people working together and provided some contrast to the sombre news from former Yugoslavia, the Middle East and other areas of conflict.

To contact as many organizations as possible, a letter inviting participation in the Year was sent out in March 1992 to religious bodies and local interfaith groups. In the letter, WCF offered to produce a handout listing events. This would help create the sense of participating in a national event. In fact, the handout became a well-produced four-page newsletter, *One Family*. The response was such that the first issue could only list events up till the end of July 1993 and it was necessary to produce four issues. *One Family* has continued to be published three times a year. An envelope sticker advertising 1993 also proved popular.

## Local events

Events took place up and down the country and were very varied in character. Bristol, which anticipated the national launch with its own launch nine days earlier, had monthly meetings for which each faith in turn took responsibility. The Lord Mayor, as well as the Bishop of Bristol, attended the Bristol launch and subsequently the Mayor arranged his own event at the City Hall. The mayors of several other cities also gave their support to the Year.

Most local interfaith groups and councils reported that events were better supported than usual. There does seem to have been some quickening of interest. A number of people met with and talked to people of other faiths for the first time. Many events included a shared meal and a cultural programme. This is evidence of a growing recognition that difference is a gift, not a threat. British life today is enriched by its wide variety of peoples, cultures and religions.

Some events were in inner cities, others in country gardens. Many religious groups arranged special programmes. The Ramakrishna Order, whose Swami Vivekananda had played a leading role at Chicago in 1893, held a series of meetings. The Unitarian Church arranged some national events and local Unitarians were supportive of local programmes. A Methodist day conference to commemorate the Parliament was held in West Yorkshire. In Edinburgh, a day-long programme was held in the General Assembly Hall of the Church of Scotland, with a welcome from the Moderator. There were a few protestors and one wondered what John Knox, whose statue dominates the courtyard, would have made of it. The Swedenborgian Church arranged a conference in London. This was appropriate because Charles Bonney, who

HH the Dalai Lama greets Marcus Braybrooke

suggested the Chicago Parliament and was its president, had been
a Swedenborgian. Birmingham Cathedral hosted events as did St
James, Piccadilly, St-Martin-in-the-Fields, Christ Church, Bath and
a few other churches. The predominantly Anglican Modern
Churchpeople's Union, which in 1991 had held a conference on
the monotheistic religions and in 1992 on eastern religions,
devoted its 1993 conference to 'Faith Outside Faiths'. Westminster
Interfaith, which has strong Roman Catholic support, focused its
very active programme on observing the centenary. There were
special lectures or meetings at Lancaster University, at Exeter
University and at other universities and colleges. The World
Congress of Faiths' own programme, naturally enough, focused on
the Year.

The above is only a sample, but indicates the breadth of
support, although one is aware that large numbers of the
practising members of religious communities still are unaware of,
uninterested in, or opposed to interfaith activity. There was some
endorsement from acknowledged religious leaders, but still
considerable caution, HH the Dalai Lama, during his visit to
Britain, being a notable exception to this generalization. Even if
religious leaders are increasingly recognizing the importance of

interfaith co-operation, religious bodies are still very reluctant to make available the funds and resources that this work requires.

## The launch

Although the emphasis for the Year of Inter-religious Understanding and Co-operation was on local activity, it was agreed to arrange a major national event to launch the Year. The hope was that this would create public awareness and would encourage and inspire those planning local events.

A committee widely representative of the faith communities in Britain was convened to plan the launch. The first meeting of the committee was held on 22 April 1992. It was encouraging that almost all those invited attended the meeting, chaired by Lord Ennals with great charm and skill. Lord Ennals gave a great deal of time to the detailed planning of the event. Whilst not identified with a particular religious community, he was a spiritual person. This was significant because from the beginning it was hoped that the launch would not be a gathering for an 'inter-religious in-group', but would speak to many in British society, uninvolved with institutional religions, but with a deep concern for spiritual and moral values. This was why the programme included participants from many walks of life.

The launch, held at Global Co-operation House at the invitation of the Brahma Kumaris World Spiritual University, on 27 January 1993, was a day-long event. It fell into three parts. The morning was fairly formal; the afternoon was spent in workshops; and the evening was a cultural celebration. I have described the launch quite fully in *Faith in a Global Age*, so here I will summarize the main components of the day.[4]

The morning began with welcomes from Lord Ennals and Dadi Janki, additional administrative head of the Brahma Kumaris World Spiritual University. There were addresses from Bishop Trevor Huddleston, known for his long campaign against apartheid, Dr Mai Yamani, a social anthropologist who gave a very clear exposition of Islam's concern for a society based on moral values, Swami Bhavyananda, head of the Ramakrishna Vedanta Centre in Britain, Rabbi Hugo Gryn of the West London Synagogue, and Edgar D. Mitchell, the Apollo XIV astronaut, who

Swami Bhavyananda

spoke movingly of the sense of the oneness, beauty and fragility of our planet as seen from space. That image had in fact been shown at the start of the proceedings.

To create a link with the 1893 Parliament, a lively dramatization of the 1893 Parliament was presented by Jane Lapotaire, Clarke Peters and Robin Ramsay. At the end of the morning, children from a local school, Barham Junior School, carried in a great globe on a stretcher – the world was dying and required urgent care. As the children started to rescue the world they sang, led by Marneta Viegas, Michael Jackson's 'Heal the World', whilst an enormous 'One World Quilt of Unity', made by a group in Milton Keynes, was raised as a backdrop to the stage.

The morning was punctuated by the Water Ceremony. On the stage, there was a fountain. Two members of each faith were asked together to bring a gift of water and to say a prayer. For some, the water came from a special source. The Christians brought water from the river Jordan, the Hindus from the river Ganges, the Muslims from Zamzam. Some of the prayers specifically related to water. The Christian prayer was from the Roman Catholic baptism service. From the Qur'an there was a verse which speaks of God making all things from water.

Because of the lingering suspicions that interfaith is really a new amalgamated faith, some care was taken with explaining the significance of the ceremony. The programme said:

> Each religion has treasures to share with all people. In the ceremony, representatives of each World Faith will say a prayer and offer its treasures in the form of water. The 'water' may symbolise the cleansing of the scars of conflict, the bringing of refreshment to the thirsty or the renewal of hope for a just and peaceful world where nature's bounty is valued and not polluted. The mingling of the waters symbolises how from their own rich and diverse sources faiths can come together in the service of humanity.[5]

The afternoon workshops focused on particular values but in a way that showed their relevance to world issues. This was done by the careful choice of co-ordinators and speakers, who represented a wide range of concerns and activities, including, for example, a member of the UN Department of Economic and Social Development and the president of the International Fellowship of Reconciliation. Douglas Martin, director-general of the Office of Public Information of the Bahá'í International Community in Haifa and I were asked to respond to the workshop reports.

The evening, introduced by Clarke Peters, included moving readings by Hayley Mills and by John Cleese, who chose passages from Sogyal Rinpoche's *Tibetan Book of Living and Dying* and contributions of music and song from several faith traditions. As always, children stole the show. Tibetan children from the Pestalozzi Children's Village sang and danced. Thai children also danced. A young Sikh performed a spiritual sword dance, Jain children gave us a lullaby dance and children of Forest School acted a play. There was a devotional Kathak piece by Sushmita Ghosh and music from the Bahá'í National Choir. There were closing messages by Edward Carpenter and Dadi Janki. At the end of a long day Sheila Chandra sang 'Sacred Stones', which blended in a wonderful and moving way eastern and western traditions of sacred music and, late into the evening, provided a fitting climax to the day.

The day served its purpose. Over eight hundred people participated on a working day; many of them were later to arrange local events. Some had travelled from Scotland and Wales. Some religious leaders had come from the South of France. The day was a blend of faiths, cultures and walks of life. It demonstrated the enrichment that our cultural and religious variety can bring to our life together. The launch also made clear that interfaith is not just about how religions relate to each other, but also about how together they can contribute to a divided and needy world.

## A service of thanksgiving and rededication

This theme was to be taken up in a service of thanksgiving and rededication held in the West London Synagogue to mark the conclusion of the Year. It was felt to be important that there should be a concluding event, as sometimes 'Years' just peter out.

The attendance of nearly two hundred people was much less than that for the launch, yet it was quite good for a winter evening. The service included a sermon by Bishop Tom Butler, the Bishop of Leicester, and the reading of the Introduction to the Declaration towards a Global Ethic, followed by comments on this. The service itself was for the Jewish festival of Chanukkah, which recalls the time when, in 168 BCE, Antiochus IV Epiphanes defiled the Temple in Jerusalem. It was recaptured by the Maccabees, but when they came to rededicate the Temple, only one day's supply of pure olive oil could be found. Miraculously it lasted for the eight days necessary to fetch further supplies.

The light of faith and hope lit at the World's Parliament of Religions in Chicago in 1893 has often been nearly extinguished by the bloodshed and cruelty of the twentieth century. The hope is that the Year of Inter-religious Understanding and Co-operation has passed on that light to a new century. 'Chanukkah' means dedication, and all who attended the service of thanksgiving and rededication were aware of the work that remains to be done. There is a rabbinic saying that it is not given to us to complete the work, but neither is it for us to cease from it.

# 13. *A worldwide interfaith family: international links*

Although Younghusband quickly took steps to establish the World Congress of Faiths as an international organization, the Second World War largely destroyed his efforts. Subsequently, small WCF groups have come into being in some other countries. The journal has had a small international circulation. WCF has also had friendly links with organizations with similar aims in several parts of the world, such as, in the fifties, the World Alliance for International Friendship through Religion and subsequently with the International Association for Religious Freedom, the Temple of Understanding and the World Conference on Religion and Peace.

## WCF overseas groups

### The Netherlands: Interreligio

Interreligio, founded in 1948 and then called *Wereldgesprek der Godsdiensten*, has been one of the most successful WCF groups outside Britain.

News of the 1936 World Congress of Faiths created quite a lot of interest in the Netherlands, especially among Liberal Protestants, Theosophists, Sufis and others with a real interest in eastern cultures and religions. In 1938, Sir Francis Younghusband visited the Netherlands, with the hope of arranging for a congress in the Peace Palace in The Hague. The council of the Peace Palace were, however, not enthusiastic about the idea. In any case, the outbreak of the Second World War soon made the project impossible.

After the war, the initiative to found a Dutch branch of the Congress was taken by Professor C. J. Bleeker of the University of Amsterdam, a distinguished scholar of comparative religion, and for some years secretary of the International Association for the History of Religions. When the society was officially registered on 17 November 1948, Professor Bleeker became the first chairman, with Helene Calkoen van Thienen as secretary. The objects of the

society were the furtherance of inter-religious dialogue, the
spreading of knowledge of the different religions and improving
contact between different religious communities in the
Netherlands. Lectures were held in several major cities and a
number of conferences, often with participants from other
countries, were held at the School for Philosophy at Amersfoort,
just outside Amsterdam.

The sixties and seventies saw a considerable change in the
population of the Netherlands, which was becoming a plural
society. Interreligio, as the society was now named, was devotedly
led by Dr Rudolf Boeke, whose doctoral thesis was on Rudolf
Otto. Interreligio attracted many who were not in contact with the
main religious bodies but who were concerned for spiritual values
and religious experience. It dealt with inquiries about the specific
practices of the world religions and with requests for educational
material, for speakers, and for information on new religious
developments. A quarterly magazine, *Levensteken* (Lifesign), was
started. Interreligio maintained contact with similar centres
abroad, especially through *Levensteken*, which went to about five
hundred people or institutions overseas. For a time Interreligio had
a centre in a busy street in Rotterdam, from which it provided help
for teachers of world religions and answered a wide range of
queries, and at which it arranged exhibitions. It started meetings
for those working for the media, to encourage more responsible
reporting of religious matters.

After twenty years as chairman, Dr Boeke felt the time had
come to resign. After an interregnum, his place was taken by Toja
van Dongen-Meyer, a Liberal Protestant. She was active in
organizing many lectures. She also attended a large number of
national and international conferences on behalf of Interreligio. A
good library of religious and spiritual books and magazines was
formed and housed in a rented room in the Remonstrant house in
Deventer in the east of Holland. The library room quickly became
a centre for meetings.

After nine years, Toja van Dongen-Meyer was succeeded by
the present (1995) chairman, Erik Hoogcarspel, a Buddhist and
teacher of philosophy. The number of lectures and meetings has
decreased recently, but greater importance is attached to the
journal, *Levensteken*, of which the quality and the size has been

improved. Interreligio is represented at many interfaith meetings in the Netherlands and is actively engaged in improving contacts with the various ethnic and religious groups that make up the population of the Netherlands.

## France

In France, as we have seen, a conference was held in 1939.[1] The war made any immediate follow-up impossible. In the late forties, steps were taken, with the private encouragement of Teilhard de Chardin, to establish a French branch of WCF, which became known as *L'Union des Croyants* .[2]

In her 1978 Younghusband Lecture, Professor Ursula King, now of the University of Bristol and a vice-president of WCF, spoke of Teilhard de Chardin's concept of the convergence of religions. He did not use the term in the sense of syncretism:

> In a realistic appraisal, he affirmed that religious diversity is here to stay . . . The idea of the convergence of religions is the opposite to the attitude which assumes that all religions are already one in essence . . . Unity is not pregiven, it is not reducible to something already there. Like all living things it has to grow and take shape over time. True convergence means the presence of an overall orientation, an axis along which certain developments of major importance occur.

With such a viewpoint, Teilhard de Chardin who, like Younghusband, had travelled widely, especially in China, was sympathetic to the aims of WCF.

*L'Union des Croyants* was led for many years by Comtesse de Pange, who quite often attended the annual conference in Britain. *L'Union des Croyants* for several years arranged lectures at a high scholarly level, but its activities seem now to be only occasional.

## Belgium

In Belgium, the Revd Christiaan Vonck, a Protestant clergyman, has, from small beginnings, established a Faculty for the Comparative Study of Religion at Antwerp University. Christiaan Vonck initially drew support from the World Congress of Faiths and continues to keep in touch with WCF activities. The faculty has grown steadily to become an important centre of study.

*India*

In South India, Dr Ahamed Kaber, a poet and author of *The Beacon Light to the World*, founded a branch in 1950, based in the ancient city of Madurai. As founder-president of the South Asiatic Zone of WCF, he arranged regular lectures and meetings.

**WCF tours**

Pilgrimage is part of the life of several religions. WCF was amongst the organizations to pioneer the idea of travel as a way of inter-religious meeting. Each WCF tour has included visits to a variety of religious communities.

The itinerary of the first WCF tour to India was hastily rearranged because of extensive flooding in North India. The group spent time with the Ramakrishna Mission in Calcutta and also visited Madras and Madurai, where the local WCF group arranged a memorable reception. Bernice Joachim, in her report, beautifully captured the 'intriguing kaleidoscope of colours and contrasts' of the days in India:

> We sat cross-legged on a cool stone floor of an ashram at the feet of a guru for two hours in the early morning at Poona; and wound our way through massive crowds and between or over reclining bodies beneath the blare of piped music at midday at the Meenakshi temple at Madurai; trod softly, with wonderment, between the 'thousand pillars' of the hall of the neighbouring museum with its stirring altar of flame at the far end.
>
> For a short while we shared the still attention of the simple, devoted worship at the temple of the Ramakrishna Mission at Belurmath, and with the sound of the worshippers' chanting in the background, stood on the banks of the swollen waters of

WCF Members at a reception in Madurai, India

the Ganges as it swept silently by, carrying unidentified bundles in its swirling torrents.[3]

On the second India tour, the group was warmly welcomed by the Guru Nanak Foundation in New Delhi and welcomed to the Golden Temple at Amritsar, where the Treasury of Jewels was specially opened. Many of the group travelled to Dharamsala for an audience with the Dalai Lama.

Mary Braybrooke mentioned in her report both the poverty and the exhilaration of a first visit to India:

Materially it is impossible to forget that we have so much in the West and many of them so little. Yet they have much to teach us about acceptance, about family love and hospitality – some of them about the way of non-violence.

I cannot begin to describe all we did and saw. Highlights were a visit to the Taj Mahal, as impressive as its pictures; houseboats on Lake Dal in Kashmir; watching *arti*, Hindu evening worship by the Ganges; shopping and bargaining in the bazaars; riding on an elephant in Corbett National Park; flying over the Himalayas; the ashram at Vrindaban and

Members of the second WCF tour being welcomed at the Guru Nanak
Foundation in New Delhi

unforgettably crowded street scenes of cars, buses, rickshaws,
tongas, cows and dogs – all converging.

The group was reminded of the suffering that is caused by
religious hostility: 'The Sunday before we left we attended
worship at the local Church of North India in Srinagar – burnt
down twice during Muslim rioting.'[4] Indeed memories of that
tour, with its visit to Amritsar and Kashmir, have added
poignancy to reports of subsequent troubles and suffering in
both places.

Many members of WCF also travelled to India in 1993 for
Sarva-Dharma-Sammelana and took part in the accompanying
tours.

There have also been tours to the Holy Land. The first took
place whilst George Appleton was Anglican Archbishop in
Jerusalem. He arranged an interesting interfaith conference for the
group, which stayed at a hotel on the Mount of Olives.

The second tour, which I led with Rabbi Hugo Gryn,
included Jews, Christians, Hindus and Buddhists. Amongst the
visits was one to Yad va-Shem. Jean Prickett wrote:

Members of the 1994 tour were welcomed by Bahá'ís to Bahjí, near 'Akká in Israel

This coloured for some of us all our subsequent experiences in Israel. Of course, we all *knew* about it, but I walked out into the sunlit concourse feeling hollow and numb. It was a sensitive move to take us next to see Chagall's brilliant stained glass windows of the twelve tribes of Israel in the synagogue of the Hadassah-Hebrew Medical Centre.

On our last evening, we stood in silence by the shore of the Sea of Galilee as dusk came and distant lights appeared across the water. The single plaintive call of a bird became less insistent and then ceased. A boat glided out from the bank a few yards away and the fisherman circled the boat, spreading his net.[5]

In 1994, the tour included a visit to Jordan as well as Israel. This was just after the peace agreement between Israel and the Palestinian Liberation Organization had been signed. In fact, the group left Amman on the very day that Jericho and Gaza became autonomous areas. A highlight of the tour was the welcome by the Bahá'ís to their holy places at Haifa, Bahjí and 'Akká.

In 1996, to mark the sixtieth anniversary of WCF, a tour

took place to Nepal and Tibet, where Younghusband had his decisive spiritual experience.

## Links with other interfaith organizations

In recent years, WCF has tried to discharge its international role by building up links with other interfaith bodies in different parts of the world and particularly by initiating the conferences for international interfaith organizations which led to them working together to mark 1993 as a Year of Inter-religious Understanding and Co-operation.

Friendly relations with other international groups have been developed by WCF being represented at many international gatherings. Heather McConnell and I attended the Temple of Understanding's Second Spiritual Summit Conference, held in Geneva in 1970. Bishop Appleton, K. D. D. Henderson, Mary Braybrooke and I have attended other Temple of Understanding events. Several WCF members over the years have attended Congresses of the International Association for Religious Freedom and also the Assemblies of the World Conference on Religion and Peace. Regular contact has been maintained with World Thanksgiving, which is based in Dallas.

WCF has also kept in touch with many world religious bodies and been represented at some of their gatherings. For example, I attended the Vancouver Assembly of the World Council of Churches and David and Jean Potter attended the Canberra Assembly. David and Celia Storey and others have been to several interfaith meetings in India and Mary and I have been invited to conferences in Korea and Japan as well as the USA.

Much of the lasting value of such gatherings is the friendships that are created and remain. There has slowly developed an international interfaith family. This has enriched the lives of those involved, but also provided an important channel of information and support in building up good inter-religious relations. Whilst the expression of this is often very local, the international dimension is important. What happens in one country affects relationships in another. Communal trouble in India has had repercussions in Great Britain. Violent clashes in the

Middle East have affected Christian–Muslim–Jewish relationships in Europe. Events in former Yugoslavia have caused problems for Muslims elsewhere.

## Ammerdown, April 1985

To try to strengthen the sense of partnership, WCF arranged a meeting of representatives of international interfaith organizations at the Ammerdown Conference Centre near Bath in April 1985. It was not as representative as had been hoped, being dominated by Europeans and Americans. This was partly because no funds were available to subsidize travel for participants from Asia. Even so, the major international interfaith organizations participated. A number of national organizations and some study centres were also represented.

Ammerdown is a retreat as well as a conference centre. The discussions were deliberately set in the context of quiet, meditation and prayer. Time was given to building personal relations, which are vital in interfaith work, and to describing the work of the organizations represented.

Besides recognizing the need to strengthen links between interfaith organizations, the conference suggested that the various events held to commemorate the Chicago World's Parliament of Religions might be linked and that the year 'could provide an opportunity to touch people more widely with the spirit of interfaith dialogue'.

In a rather euphoric mood, the conference warmed to the suggestion by Dr John Taylor of trying to create a 'World Council of Religions', 'to bring together people of all religions to overcome religious sectarianism, to work for peace, and to link individuals and organizations working for interfaith understanding'. Attempts to pursue this came to nothing, but the idea was mentioned again at the Parliament of the World's Religions in Chicago in 1993 and at the conference held in San Francisco in 1995 to mark the fiftieth anniversary of the signing of the Charter of the United Nations.[6]

Following Ammerdown, communication between interfaith organizations increased. WCF, the Temple of Understanding, IARF, World Thanksgiving and WCRP were invited to be represented at the World Day of Prayer for Peace at Assisi in 1986.

*Ammerdown, April 1988*

In April 1988, a second meeting of international interfaith organizations was held, again at Ammerdown. The main outcome was a call for 'world wide celebration of the centenary of the World's Parliament of Religions'. By the following January, all four organizations – IARF, the Temple of Understanding, WCF and WCRP – agreed jointly to sponsor 'a Year of Inter-religious Understanding and Co-operation' in 1993 and to hold a special centennial gathering. After considerable discussion, Bangalore was chosen as the venue.[7]

The planning body – an *ad hoc* group – became known as the International Inter-religious Co-ordinating Committee (IIOCC), with David and Celia Storey as secretaries and myself as chairperson. I had known David at college and we had met on occasion since. I was asked to speak at Chichester and had a meal with Celia Storey beforehand. David was away at Findhorn. Very quickly they became excited by the plans for 1993 and soon found themselves immersed in an enormous amount of work to make it possible.

To publicize plans for Bangalore and to link other events being planned around the world to mark the Year of Inter-religious Understanding and Co-operation, a newsletter, *Towards 1993*, was circulated. The first issue appeared at the beginning of 1991.

*India, 1993*

Besides the main conference, known as Sarva-Dharma-Sammelana, which means 'religious people coming together', there were other conferences in Bangalore, at Kanyakumari, organized by the World Fellowship of Inter-Religious Councils in which Fr Albert Nambiaparambil has played a leading part, also in Delhi, and retreats at Mt Abu and in Rishikesh.

Nearly six hundred people attended Sarva-Dharma-Sammelana, which was held at the Ashok Hotel at Bangalore. There is a full record of the conference in *Visions of an Interfaith Future*.[8]

The whole conference was set in a context of prayer and

L to R: Cherry Gould, Dr Jeremy Braybrooke, HE the Governor of Karnataka and the Archbishop of Bangalore at the opening of Sarva-Dharma-Sammelana in 1993

meditation. Indeed in the hotel garden, where many events took place, there was a tree under which Gandhi used regularly to spend time in meditation when he was in Bangalore.

The conference began with a joyful and prayerful opening ceremony. This started with the lighting of a lamp by Cherry Gould, a member of WCF, and by various religious dignitaries. There were prayers from each tradition; I gave a message of welcome; Dr N. Mahalingam, president of the Ramalinga Mission, gave the keynote address; and the main address was given by HE Kursheed Alam Khan, the governor of the state of Karnataka.

The final ceremony, arranged by the younger participants, was also a joyous and prayerful occasion. Each day participants came together in the morning and evening for times of prayer and meditation, led by members of one faith community.

There were three programmes. One involved intensive small-group work in which participants produced a shared vision of interfaith co-operation. The second consisted of visits to a large number of local religious centres. In the third programme, there were seven workshops on key issues, such as 'Education for Understanding' or 'Service and Solidarity'.

L to R: Shri P. V. Narasimha Rao, Prime Minister of India, the Revd
Marcus Braybrooke, the Revd Naganuma and the Revd Dr Robert Traer

In the evening there were cultural programmes, some
hosted by local communities. These allowed many of the citizens
of Bangalore to share in some of Sarva-Dharma-Sammelana.
The governor kindly arranged a reception at Raj Bhavan for all
the delegates.

One Japanese participant, who had been afraid to come to
India because of reports of communal trouble, said of Sarva-
Dharma-Sammelana that it was a foretaste of paradise, with the
blue skies, beautiful flowers, butterflies and smiling faces
everywhere. Certainly, my own lasting memory is of the warmth of
the friendships and the sheer enjoyment of our rich variety. It was
primarily a gathering for those involved in interfaith work and
gave them the chance to share their achievements, their failures
and their hopes. It showed that in all their diversity, those
committed to inter-religious understanding and co-operation have
become an international family and are a symbol of hope to a
world still scarred by ethnic and religious conflict.

In Delhi there was a day centennial meeting, at which Dr

1993 celebrations in Japan

Karan Singh, a former member of the Indian government and chairman of the Temple of Understanding, presided and gave a keynote address. The highlight was a speech from Shri P. V. Narasimha Rao, the Prime Minister of India, who stressed that India's constitution gave equal respect to all faiths.

*Worldwide*

There were other international gatherings to mark the centenary of the World's Parliament of Religions, especially in Japan and at Chicago itself. Dr Daniel Gómez-Ibáñez, the executive director of the Chicago Parliament, attended several meetings of IIOCC and has become a good friend. Mary and I were privileged to represent WCF both in Japan and at Chicago. Several other WCF members, including Sir Sigmund and Lady Sternberg, David and Celia Storey and Brian Pearce, were present at Chicago.

## An international interfaith centre

Many who took part in the Year of Inter-religious Understanding and Co-operation have felt it was important to maintain the links that have been built up. A number of new initiatives are being explored. There is a continuing organization at Chicago, concerned with work both in the metropolitan area and internationally. A Peace Council, of which Dr Daniel Gómez Ibáñez is now executive director, held its first meeting at Windsor at the end of November 1995. A United Religions Organization has been proposed by Bishop Swing of California, following celebrations to mark the fiftieth anniversary of the signing of the UN Charter in San Francisco. Existing international interfaith organizations are increasing their programmes.[9]

The World Congress of Faiths has been particularly involved in the establishment of an international interfaith centre at Oxford. The energies that were channelled into its international committee are now invested in the centre.

For some time before 1993, IARF and WCF had been in conversation about the need for such a centre. After careful consultation, it was agreed that Oxford would be a very suitable venue and Westminster College, which has a strong department for the study of religions, agreed to co-operate with the project. By the end of 1993, both the International Association for Religious Freedom and the World Congress of Faiths had relocated their offices to Oxford.[10]

In December 1993, a trust deed was signed to establish the International Interfaith Centre (IIC) at Oxford, which is now a registered charity.

The objects of the Centre are:

To advance the education of the public worldwide in its understanding of the different faith traditions and various faith communities and how they might live in harmony, by establishing a Centre to promote or assist research into:

1. issues of interfaith understanding, co-operation and religious freedom;
2. teaching methods and the development of educational

A model of the design for the International Interfaith Centre, Oxford, by Evans and Shalev [Eamon O'Mahony]

materials;
3. aspects of worship, prayer, meditation and spiritual discipline;
and to disseminate the useful results of such research.

Already the Centre has held three international conferences. The first, in April 1994, was on 'Religious Practice, Justice and Transformation'. It took a critical look at the effectiveness of religion in helping to make society more just. There was discussion of the patterns of religious education in several countries. The second, in April 1995, was on 'Threat or Promise? The Study of Religions and Interfaith Activity'. There was again sober analysis of what interfaith organizations could do in areas of conflict. In 1996, the theme was 'Interfaith Achievements? Initiatives around the World', with sessions on interfaith work in Sri Lanka, the Middle East and on the position of indigenous people in the Americas.

Lectures on the relation of religions to the environmental crisis have been give by Dr Seyyed Hossein Nasr of George Washington University, by Professor Seshagiri Rao of the University of Virginia, and by Dr Paul Knitter of Xavier University, Cincinnati. Reports of the conferences and lectures are contained in *International Interfaith News*.

Visits to faith communities and educational centres in or near to Oxford have been arranged, including the Postgraduate Centre for Hebrew Studies at Yarnton, Keston College and the Oxford Centre for Islamic Studies. Other visits have provided an opportunity to learn about different aspects of worship, prayer, meditation and spiritual discipline.

In its first two and a half years, the centre has received a steady stream of visitors, who have come to seek advice and information. Several have been staff members of international or national interfaith organizations or of world religious bodies. Others have been scholars in this field. A far greater number of enquiries have come by letter, telephone, fax and e-mail.

The co-ordinators, Celia Storey and Sandy Martin, have already collected information on major international interfaith organizations and multireligious world bodies. Information is also held about many national and local interfaith organizations and is being gathered on major faith communities and their structures for interfaith relations, and also about major academic centres for the study of religions. A programme of research is being developed.

The architects, Evans and Shalev, who have designed a number of distinctive buildings, have prepared an initial design for the Centre. A fund-raising campaign for the building and endowment fund, under the guidance of Neville Sandelson, a former Member of Parliament, has been launched. HRH Prince Charles has written a message of support and Sir Richard Greenbury, chairman of Marks and Spencer, has agreed to be president of the appeal.

The preparations for the Year of Inter-religious Understanding and Co-operation and the travel involved have shown me how many people in different parts of the world are working for inter-religious understanding, human rights, peace, the relief of the hungry and the preservation of the planet. As I said in my welcome at Bangalore:

The flowing together of so many streams of new life will create a river strong enough to wash away the stains of ethnic cleansing, racism, sexism, discrimination, communalism and apartheid. Many people long for renewal, for a world rebuilt on spiritual principles. What is necessary is that those who share this hope should share their energies.[11]

The International Interfaith Centre is intended to facilitate such sharing, to carry forward the achievements of the Year of Inter-religious Understanding and Co-operation and to be a step towards fulfilling Akbar's dream of a place where 'Truth and Peace and Love and Justice came and dwelt'.[12]

# 14. 'In the Great Unity, We are Members One of Another': conclusion

The World Congress of Faiths has not become the world organization that Sir Francis Younghusband dreamed of, yet there is now a worldwide movement for inter-religious understanding. The World Congress of Faiths has also not gained large popular support, yet there has been a significant shift in attitudes about the relation of religions to each other.

## A changing world

It is never easy to assess the achievements of an organization concerned with public education. A full study would require more detailed analysis both of the changing social and political scene and of theological developments.

Younghusband, as we have seen, has been described by his biographer as the 'last great imperial adventurer'. By the time the Congress met in 1936, albeit unbeknown to the participants, the days of the British Empire were numbered. Many who enthusiastically supported the Congress, however, had been schooled in imperial service and were deeply interested in the various religious beliefs and practices of those who belonged to the Empire.

In the years after the Second World War, the number of people in Britain who retained this world concern declined. Interest in world religions was a minority pursuit. It was not until the mid seventies that religious and political leaders in Britain began to become aware of the growing Muslim, Hindu and Sikh communities in some of Britain's larger cities.

Even then, with the decline of church-going, there was a widespread feeling that religion was a matter for the individual in his or her private life. The social importance of the fact that Britain was becoming multireligious as well as multiracial and multicultural was largely ignored.

It was not until the late eighties that the relevance of religions to social and political life began to be recognized, even by those who were not personally committed members of a faith community. This was for two reasons. One was negative, as people suddenly woke up to the divisive power of religious extremism and inter-religious hostility not only in the Lebanon or Sri Lanka but, after the Salman Rushdie affair, in Britain itself. Recent tragic events in former Yugoslavia and the evidence of increasing anti-Semitism and xenophobia in many parts of Europe have confirmed how serious a threat religious extremism is to social stability. Whereas at one time religious news in the papers mostly consisted of stories about clergy caught up in sexual scandal, now most serious newspapers give careful coverage to developments in the lives of the different faith communities. Religion is seen, for good or ill, to have an impact on the life of the whole community.

The positive reason for renewed attention to religion is the growing recognition that the major issues that face humanity, such as how to provide for the millions who are starving in poverty or how to protect the environment or questions of genetic engineering, have a profound spiritual and moral dimension. With the collapse of communism, the United Nations in its many programmes can now acknowledge the relevance of spiritual and ethical concerns. Further, the recognition that so many problems are global has encouraged more people to think in world terms and to recognize that the involvement of religious people in public debate has to be multireligious.

This new situation, both in world and national terms, means that there is a wider recognition today by those who shape public opinion, even if they are themselves not religious, of the importance of the sort of work that the World Congress of Faiths has been trying to do for sixty years.

Much of the work is in fact being done by other bodies. Members of WCF could be excused for feeling a little jealous of newcomers to the scene who have grown more rapidly. Yet the purpose of WCF has never been to create a large organization but to change the attitude of members of the great religions to each other.

The fact that many members of one religion now look on members of other religions as friends rather than as enemies is the sign of a considerable alteration in religious relationships to which

WCF, along with other groups, has made a valuable contribution. At the leadership level of many faith communities, there has been a dramatic change of attitude over the last sixty years, but this has been matched, in other quarters, by a dangerous increase of religious extremism and hostility. The work of bodies such as WCF now has the endorsement of many religious leaders at a time when the evils of religious extremism are all too apparent. It is by no means clear either in Britain or on the world scene whether the future lies with inter-religious understanding and co-operation or with religious rivalry and hatred. What is clear is the enormous consequences of the path that is chosen – consequences summed up in the slogan 'dialogue or die'.

## A pioneering body

WCF has been a pioneering body. Its influence is partly to be seen in the establishment of organizations specializing in concerns to which WCF was amongst the first to draw attention. WCF, as we have seen, from its early days, voiced the need for the study of world religions in universities and schools. The change in the shape of religious education in the last fifty years has been remarkable. WCF was probably the first organization to arrange occasions at which people of different religions could pray together. Fifty years after the first Congress, the Pope invited leaders of the world's religions to the World Day of Prayer for Peace at Assisi. Interfaith prayer has now become quite a widespread, if still controversial, practice. WCF started a few local interfaith groups. Now there are such groups in most parts of Britain. In the eighties, WCF brought together international interfaith organizations. Now plans are well developed to establish an international interfaith centre. More examples of WCF's pioneering role can be seen by looking back at previous chapters. This is not to claim all the credit for WCF. Many others, including theologians and scholars in the study of religions, have helped create a changed awareness about the relationship of religions to each other. It is, however, to acknowledge WCF's influence, even if in organizational terms WCF remains very fragile. Some years ago the BBC's religious affairs correspondent Douglas Brown, rightly in my opinion, spoke of the World Congress of Faiths as a 'comparatively small but very significant' body.[1]

Today, WCF continues its pioneering role. It is, for example, stimulating reflection between members of different religions about the nature of multifaith prayer. It is also encouraging discussion of the sensitive issues surrounding mixed-faith marriages. Both of these are controversial but important subjects. WCF has also recognized that interfaith concerns now have an impact on many aspects of life and are not just of interest to religious professionals. For example, WCF has arranged conferences to look at how people of different faiths in the caring professions should minister to the elderly and to the dying. WCF has also given attention to questions about the possibility of recognizing moral values shared by members of the world religions.

The value of WCF's work will depend on the quality of its contribution to the discussion of important issues. This suggests that instead of the large conferences of the seventies, WCF's meetings may be smaller and more focused on particular topics. The discussion should also be followed up by working parties and the preparation of publications. Already WCF has a great asset in its journal.

It has always been difficult to attract significant funding for such pioneering work, although sometimes it can be found for specific projects. This is why WCF has throughout its history been so dependent on voluntary effort. It may also be that WCF's membership has remained quite small, not only because WCF has been poor at publicity and self-promotion, but also because its outlook has been ahead of its time. Many of its members have been highly gifted and original people, who had a wider vision.

## A wider vision

It is this wider vision that perhaps is still a distinctive characteristic of WCF. There are many good reasons to recognize the importance of understanding and co-operation between members of different faith communities, such as the evident suffering caused by religious prejudice, the need to live together harmoniously in a multifaith society, a desire to understand our neighbours' beliefs and practices, the search for shared values and the hope that people of different religions can together address the urgent challenges that face our world. Such concerns have inspired different members of WCF. They all, however, at their deepest, spring from a sense of a common humanity and of a spiritual unity that transcends religious particularity. In the presence of the Ultimate Mystery all are at one.

This is why WCF has had to be a fellowship of like-minded individuals, albeit of different religions, rather than a body consisting of representatives of particular faith communities. For the discovery of the wider vision is intensely personal and has been called a second conversion – the first conversion being to a living faith. Kathleen de Beaumont wrote:

> The basic fact of our spiritual attainment is and must be an individual one. The awakening to the spiritual life becomes a reality when man of his own free will opens wide his soul, when he becomes attuned to those divine vibrations within and around him of which for so long he has remained unconscious – when the flood of Being possesses him and he becomes aware of union with his Source.[2]

That union also inspires a sense of unity with others, whatever their religious label. 'We believe', Kathleen de Beaumont continued, 'that, in the Great Unity, we are members one of another.'[3]

Many of those who have played a significant part in the life and work of WCF have had some such personal spiritual experience, which Archbishop Runcie described in words borrowed from Paul Tillich:

> In the depth of every religion there is a point at which religion itself loses its importance and that to which it points breaks through its particularity, elevating it to spiritual freedom and to a vision of the spiritual presence in other expressions of the ultimate meaning of man's existence.[4]

This is not the only motive for seeking inter-religious dialogue, but it gives a distinctive feel to the contribution WCF has made and continues to make to the very varied interfaith movement. This is why the growth of other interfaith organizations, many more powerful and better organized, has not replaced the need for the World Congress of Faiths to provide a fellowship for all, of whatever religion, who have sensed with Dean Inge that God does not mind whether He is called Dieu or Allah or Brahma or even Bog.

The emphasis in the early days of the World Congress of Faiths was on the transcendent unity. Today the richness of diversity is equally appreciated. Yet still, WCF, as a fellowship of people of faith working together for peace, justice, the relief of need and the preservation of the planet, is nourished by spiritual experience of communion with the Ultimate – an experience in which human barriers are dissolved. It is this experience that WCF has sought to embody in its fellowship and in its varied activities. The Congress continues, as Younghusband hoped, 'to awaken a wider consciousness and to offer people a vision of a happier world-order in which the roots of fellowship strike down deep to the Central Source of all spiritual loveliness'.[5]

# Notes

a. From a hymn by F. W. Faber, 'Souls of Men', *Hymns Ancient and Modern*, No. 364.

b. The quotation in the Preface is from Arnold Toynbee, 'End and Beginning' in *The Observer*, 24 October 1954.

## 1 Beginnings

1. From Alfred, Lord Tennyson's *Akbar's Dream*. I am grateful to Shelagh James for finding this quotation for me.
2. Queen Victoria, quoted by R. A. Butler in an address to WCF at Caxton Hall on 4 June 1943 in the WCF archives.
3. See Kenneth Cracknell, *Justice, Courtesy and Love* (Epworth Press, 1995).
4. This is the sub-heading to Patrick French's full and vivid biography, *Younghusband* (HarperCollins Publishers, 1994). There are several references below to this book.
5. *Religions of Empire*, ed. William Loftus Hare (Duckworth, 1925), pp. 18–19. See also the *Manchester Guardian* report for 23 September 1924.
6. Ramsay MacDonald. File of press cuttings in WCF archives, 9/1.
7. *Religions of Empire*, p. 3.
8. Report in *The Observer*, 14 September 1924.
9. *Evening News*, 6 September 1924.
10. *Religions of Empire*, p. 4.
11. Ibid., p. 3.
12. *Manchester Guardian*, 23 September 1924.
13. *The Record*, 25 September 1924.
14. Marcus Braybrooke, *Pilgrimage of Hope* (SCM Press, 1992).
15. *World Fellowship. Addresses and Messages by Leading Spokesmen of all Faiths, Races and Countries*, ed. Charles Frederick Weller (Liveright Publishing Co., 1935), p. 536. I have given a summary of the Second Parliament in Marcus Braybrooke, *Inter-Faith Organizations, 1893–1979* (Edwin Mellen Press, 1980), pp. 167–70.
16. *World Fellowship*, p. 10.
17. Ibid., p. 59.

## 2 Francis Younghusband

1. Lord (Herbert) Samuel in a BBC broadcast soon after Younghusband's death. The text is in the WCF archives.
2. Sir John Squire, 'A Man of Action and Ideas', *The Illustrated London News*, 7 March 1953.
3. Dame Eileen Younghusband, 'My Father As I Knew Him', *World Faiths*, No. 65, Spring 1966, p. 2. See also French, *Younghusband*, p. 342.
4. Dame Eileen Younghusband, 'My Father', pp. 3–4.
5. BBC broadcast by Francis Younghusband in 1936. *The Listener*, 24 June 1936, p. 1195.

6. Quoted by K. D. D. Henderson in 'Francis Younghusband and the Mysticism of Shared Endeavour', 1976 Younghusband Lecture (WCF, 1976), p. 9.
7. Chairman's speech at the WCF AGM, December 1940.
8. Inaugural address to WCF Paris conference, 1939.
9. WCF archives.
10. Francis Younghusband, *Vital Religion* (John Murray, 1940), pp. 3–5.
11. Quoted in George Harrison's unpublished 'A Younghusband Anthology of Divine Fellowship'.
12. Quoted by George Harrison, 'World Fellowship through Religion', *World Faiths*, No. 56, April 1963, p. 5.
13. The Younghusband Collection, India Office Library, MSS EUR F 197/123.
14. Ibid. From a talk in New York on 18 April 1935.
15. Ibid. Interview in *Great Thought* by R. L. Megroz, August 1936.
16. French, *Younghusband*, p. 7.
17. Quoted in George Seaver, *Francis Younghusband* (John Murray, 1952), p. 14.
18. Ibid., pp. 97–100.
19. French, *Younghusband*, p. 109.
20. Ibid., p. 119.
21. Ibid., p. 295.
22. Quoted in Seaver, *Younghusband*, p. 274.
23. *Vital Religion*, p. 4.
24. French, *Younghusband*, p. 295.
25. Ibid., p. 318.
26. Squire, 'A Man of Action and Ideas'.
27. Henderson, 'Mysticism', pp. 6–7.
28. Quoted from *The Times Literary Supplement* by George Harrison in 'World Fellowship Through Religion', p. 2.
29. Harrison, ibid., p. 3.
30. *Pilgrimage of Hope*, p. 65, quoting from *Vital Religion*, p. 17.
31. The Younghusband Collection, MSS EUR F 197/119. Notes for a talk at Westerham, Kent, p. 11.
32. Quoted in Arthur Peacock, *Fellowship through Religion* (WCF, 1956), pp. 12–13.

## 3 The 1936 Congress

1. The Younghusband Collection, MSS EUR F 197/119.
2. Minute book in WCF archives.
3. Ibid.
4. Lambeth Palace archives. Letter from Buckingham Palace of 5 May 1936 and reply to Commander Campbell from the Archbishop of 6 May 1936.
5. Lambeth Palace archives, letters of 17 June 1936 and the Archbishop's reply of 19 June 1936 and the King's message, 3 July 1936 in the WCF archives.
6. French, *Younghusband*, p. 369.
7. Ibid., p. 368.
8. The papers are printed in *Faiths and Fellowship* (J. M. Watkins, 1936

or 1937 [no date of publication is given], p. 24.

9. Ibid., p. 47.
10. Ibid., pp. 75ff.
11. Ibid., pp. 104ff.
12. Ibid., p. 151.
13. Ibid., p. 268.
14. Ibid., p. 131.
15. Ibid., p. 224.
16. Ibid., p. 422.
17. Ibid., pp. 365ff.
18. *Vital Religion*, p. 93.

## 4 1936–42

1. *The World's Need of Religion* (Nicholson & Watson, 1937).
2. *The Renascence of Religion* (published for WCF by Arthur Probsthain, 1938).
3. Paris conference: Louis Massignon.
4. Paris conference: Baron Palmstierna.
5. Chairman's circular letter, No. 6, May 1940.
6. The Younghusband Collection, MSS EUR F 197/120, WCF 1939 AGM.
7. Chairman's circular letter, No. 8, Summer 1940.
8. The Younghusband Collection, MSS EUR F 197/120.
9. Chairman's circular letter, No. 1, October 1939.
10. Chairman's circular letter, No. 9, October 1940.
11. Bedford College 1940 Conference Report, WCF archives.
12. *Church Times*, 1940, cutting in WCF archives.
13. The Younghusband Collection, MSS EUR F 197/124.
14. Chairman's circular letter, No. 11, February 1941.
15. Chairman's circular letter, No. 13, October 1941.
16. The Younghusband Collection, MSS EUR F 197/123.
17. Ibid., MSS EUR F 197/120.
18. French, *Younghusband*, p. 394.

## 5 1942–52

1. Heather McConnell, *The Times*, 14 February 1966.
2. Palmstierna's first chairman's letter and at the AGM of 10 December 1942.
3. Typescript of meeting, WCF archives.
4. Ibid. The name of the poet quoted by R. A. Butler is not given in the report.
5. Press cuttings and WCF minutes, WCF archives, and the Bell papers in the Lambeth Palace archives.
6. See Marcus Braybrooke, *Children of One God* (Vallentine Mitchell, 1991), p. 29.
7. WCF executive committee minutes, 22 May 1945.
8. WCF archives.
9. Minutes of AGM, 19 February 1948, WCF archives.
10. R. G. Coulson, *I Am* (Tunnicliffe & Paice [ISBN 0 95035005 3 2], no

date), p. 63.

11. Ibid., pp. 65ff.

12. John Stewart-Wallace, 'The Shape of Religion to Come', *The Contemporary Review*, August 1948.

13. John Stewart-Wallace, 'Religion and the Philosophy of Synthesis', *The Hibbert Journal*, April 1950.

14. WCF archives.

15. See, for example, Hendrik Kraemer, *The Christian Message in a Non-Christian World* (Edinburgh House Press, 1938) and *Religion and the Christian Faith* (Lutterworth, 1956).


## 6 1952–67

1. *The Times*, 3 February 1959.

2. *The Times*, 31 March 1980. See also the discussion of Dr Runcie's Younghusband Lecture in chapter 8.

3. A. C. Bouquet, *The Sacred Books of the World* (Penguin, 1954).

4. General Introduction by M. A. C. Warren to William Stewart's *India's Religious Frontier* (SCM Press, 1964).

5. W. W. Matthews, *Forum*, No. 47, December 1960, pp. 1–4.

6. Report in *The Christian Century*, 15 March 1956.

7. French, *Younghusband*, p. 365.

8. Elizabeth Barrett Browning, quoted in *Fellowship through Religion*.

9. WCF archives.

10. Ibid.

11. Reg Sorensen, *I Believe in Man* (Lindsey Press, 1970), p. 120.

12. *World Faiths*, No. 77, Autumn 1969, pp. 18–20.


## 7 1967–96

1. Appleton papers, WCF archives.

2. Ibid. See also 'Opportunity Knocks', *World Faiths*, No. 80, Summer 1970, pp. 3–8.

3. George Appleton, *Unfinished* (Collins, 1987), p. 16.

4. *World Faiths*, No. 101, Spring 1977, p. 4.

5. Letters by Archbishop Ramsey, 25 October 1969 and 17 November 1969 and by Edward Carpenter, 7 November 1969, WCF archives.

6. Cyclostyled report by the Revd Jack Austin, WCF archives.

7. Lesley Matthias, report to the WCF executive, WCF archives. See also *World Faiths Encounter*, No. 3, November 1992, pp. 34–40.

8. Report by Elizabeth Montgomery Campbell in the WCF archives, 17/3.

9. Report by Nikki de Carteret in the WCF archives, 2/6.

10. Report by Pauline Astor, WCF archives.


## 8 Conferences and lectures

1. *World Faiths*, No. 65, Spring 1966, p. 9.

2. *Forum*, No. 9, June 1951, pp. 7–8.

3. Ibid., p. 1.

4. Report by M. O'c. Walshe, *Forum*, No. 35, December 1957, pp. 3–7.

5. *World Faiths*, No. 77, Autumn 1969. See above, pp. 77–8.

6. Ibid., Nos. 101 and 102.
7. *World Faiths Insight*, New Series 22, June 1989.
8. *World Faiths*, No. 110, Spring 1980.
9. *World Faiths Insight*, New Series 16 and 17, June and October 1987.
10. Ibid., New Series 22–4, June and October 1989 and February 1990.
11. *World Faiths*, No. 99, Summer 1976, pp. 22–3.
12. *One Family*, Summer 1994.
13. *World Faiths Insight*, New Series 8, January 1984, p. 33.
14. Quoted in *A Journey in Faith*, WCF pamphlet and notes by Tom Gulliver and Dorothy Thomasson.
15. In *Westminster Interfaith*, July 1995.
16. *World Faiths Insight*, New Series 6, January 1983.
17. *World Faiths*, No. 20, October 1988.
18. Ibid., No. 13, June 1986.
19. Ibid., No. 12, February 1986.
20. Ibid., No. 14, October 1986.
21. Ibid., No. 22, June 1989.
22. *World Faiths Insight*, New Series 16, June 1987.

## 9 Interfaith prayer

1. *Church Times*, 19 November 1869, reproduced in the paper one hundred years later.
2. There is a growing literature on this subject and it is fully discussed in WCF's forthcoming resource book on multifaith prayer, *All in Good Faith*. See also *Multi-Faith Worship?* (Church House Publishing, 1992).
3. *The Listener*, 24 June 1936, p. 1195.
4. Will Hayes, *A Book of Twelve Services*, 1924. Some of the services are reproduced in Will Hayes, *Every Nation Kneeling* (Order of the Great Companions, 1954).
5. French, *Younghusband*, p. 398.
6. Ibid.
7. See *Forum*, No. 16, March 1953, p. 1. and No. 17, June 1953, p. 1.
8. Sermon at Great St Mary's 24 September 1967. See *World Faiths*, No. 71, Winter 1967, pp. 13ff.
9. See Marcus Braybrooke, *Inter-Faith Worship* (Galliard, 1974), p. 5.
10. Ibid., pp. 5–6.
11. WCF statement in WCF archives.
12. George Appleton, *World Faiths*, No. 81, Autumn 1970, pp. 13–19.
13. The order of service arranged with Donald Swann is reproduced as Appendix One of *Inter-Faith Worship*, pp. 15–20.
14. The titles of the reports are: 'Interfaith Services and Worship' in *Ends and Odds*, No. 22, March 1980; *Can We Pray Together?* (British Council of Churches, 1983); *Multi-Faith Worship?* (Church House Publishing, 1992).
15. Details from the Week of Prayer for World Peace, Whispering Trees, 273 Beechings Way, Rainham, Gillingham, Kent ME8 7BP.
16. *One Family*, Nos. 8 and 9, 1995.
17. *Religions of Empire*, pp. 18–19.

## 10 Publications

1. Memorandum by Heather McConnell, July 1974, in WCF archives.
2. *Forum*, No. 44, March 1960, pp. 7–8.
3. *World Faiths*, No. 48, March 1961, p. 10.
4. Ibid., No. 100, Autumn 1976.
5. Ibid., p. 31.
6. Ibid., p. 13.
7. *World Faiths Encounter*, No. 1.
8. *Interfaith News*, No. 3, Autumn 1983.
9. Ibid., No. 12, October 1986.
10. Ibid., No. 25, February 1991.
11. Marcus Braybrooke, *Faiths in Fellowship* (WCF, 1976).
12. *Faiths and Fellowship*; *The World's Need of Religion*; *Renascence of Religion*.
13. Peacock, *Fellowship Through Religion*.

## 11 Working with others

1. Kathleen de Beaumont, *My Memoirs* (privately published, no date, but about 1964), pp. 23–6.
2. Ibid., p. 36.
3. Ibid., p. 38.
4. *Cambridge Daily News*, 26 July 1954.
5. French, *Younghusband*, pp. 399–400.
6. *World Faiths Insight*, New Series 16, June 1987, p. 39.
7. *World Faiths Encounter*, No. 4, March 1993, pp. 43–51.
8. *Religions in the UK: A Multi-Faith Directory*, ed. Paul Weller (University of Derby, 1993).
9. Memorandum of 26 June 1978, quoted in *Pilgrimage of Hope*, p. 89.
10. Recommendation to AGM from WCF executive committee, 15 March 1986.
11. From the Introduction to *The Handbook* of the Inter Faith Network of the UK, 5–7 Tavistock Place, London WC1H 9SS.
12. *1994–5 Annual Report*, p. 2.
13. *World Faiths*, No. 48, March 1961, pp. 15–17.
14. Ibid., No. 73, 1968, p. 24.
15. Bernard Cousins, *Introducing Children to World Religions* (CCJ, 1965).
16. *World Faiths*, No. 62, March 1965, p. 11.
17. Ibid., No. 81, 1970, p. 20.
18. Ibid., No. 86, 1972.
19. *Initiation Rites*; *Death*; *Marriage and the Family*; all edited by John Prickett (Lutterworth, 1978, 1980 and 1985). The contact address is 88a Brondesbury Villas, Kilburn, London NW6 6AD.
20. SHAP, c/o National Society, 23 Kensington Square, London W8 5HN.
21. Religious Education Council, 1 Raffin Park, Datchworth, Herts SG3 6RR.
22. The British Association for the Study of Religions, Department of Theology and Religious Studies, University of Leeds, LS2 9TJ.
23. The International Sacred Literature Trust, 6 Mount Street, Manchester M2 5NS.

## 12 1993 in Britain

1. *Pilgrimage of Hope.*
2. *A Study for 1993* (Braybrooke Press, 1992).
3. *The Independent*, 9 January 1993.
4. For a fuller account see Marcus Braybrooke, *Faith in a Global Age* (Braybrooke Press, 1995).
5. Programme for the launch of 1993 as a Year of Inter-religious Understanding and Co-operation.

## 13 International links

1. See above, p. 50.
2. Ursula King, 'Exploring Convergence: The Contribution of World Faiths', *World Faiths*, No. 106, Autumn 1978, p. 7.
3. *World Faiths*, No. 107, Spring 1979.
4. In an article for *The Spring*, the ecumenical magazine of the churches in Wells, Somerset, 1981.
5. *World Faiths*, No. 111, Summer 1980.
6. *Pilgrimage of Hope*, p. 299.
7. Ibid., p. 302.
8. *Visions of an Interfaith Future*, eds. David and Celia Storey, (International Interfaith Centre, Oxford). I give a personal impression of the events in *Faith in a Global Age*.
9. Council for a Parliament of the World's Religions, PO Box 1630, Chicago, IL 60690-1630, USA.
   International Committee for the Peace Council, W9643 Rucks Road, Cambridge, Wisconsin 53523, USA.
   United Religions Organization, 1055 Taylor Street, San Francisco, CA 94108, USA.
10. The address of the IARF and WCF offices and of the International Interfaith Centre is 2 Market Street, Oxford OX1 3EF.
11. *Visions of an Interfaith Future*, p. 25.
12. From Alfred, Lord Tennyson's *Akbar's Dream*. See page 9.

## 14 Conclusion

1. Douglas Brown, *Church Times*, 2 December 1983, p. 12.
2. Kathleen de Beaumont, *Forum*, No. 21, June 1954, p. 21.
3. Ibid.
4. The quotation is from Paul Tillich, *Christianity and the Encounter of World Religions* (Columbia University Press, 1963), p. 97.
5. Quoted in Peacock, *Fellowship through Religion*, pp. 12–13.

# Index

(Numbers in bold indicate appearance in photographs)